You are cordially invited . . .

to enjoy social situations more.

to feel comfortable at home, at school, while traveling or just hanging out with family and friends.

to be at ease anywhere.

to be capable of handling any situation that comes your way.

Emily Post Talks with Teens About Manners and Etiquette covers it all—from talking with people to talking on the phone; from table settings to table manners; from getting along at home to how to act in public; from entertaining to being entertained; from managing money to earning money.

You are cordially invited to continue reading.

Also by Elizabeth L. Post

Emily Post's Etiquette, 14th edition

Emily Post's Complete Book of Wedding Etiquette

Emily Post's Wedding Planner

The Complete Book of Entertaining
(with Anthony Staffieri)

Please, Say Please

EMILY POST TALKS WITH TEENS ABOUT MANNERS AND ETIQUETTE

ELIZABETH L. POST
and JOAN M. COLES

Illustrations by Jill Weber

1817

Harper & Row, Publishers, New York

Grand Rapids, Philadelphia, St. Louis, San Francisco
London, Singapore, Sydney, Tokyo, Toronto

Designer: C. Linda Dingler

Library of Congress Cataloging-in-Publication Data

Post, Elizabeth L.
  Emily Post talks with teens about manners and etiquette.

  Includes index.
  1. Etiquette for children and youth. I. Coles, Joan M. II. Title.
BJ1857.C5P62 1986   395'.123   86-45135
ISBN 0-06-181685-X
ISBN 0-06-096117-1 (pbk.)

90 91 HC 10 9 8 7 6 5

90 91 HC 10 9 8 7 6 5 4 3 (ppbk)

Contents

Introduction

How many times in the past few months have you been in a situation where you felt uncomfortable? Have there been times when you wished you knew what was expected of you, what you were supposed to wear or how you were expected to look?

Everyone has experienced these awkward moments—being introduced to someone and suffering through the awkward silence that follows because you don't know what to say, showing up at a party inappropriately dressed, not knowing how much or whether to tip the waiter, dropping a fork on the floor and not knowing whether to pick it up or leave it there.

Now you may be wondering, "What does any of this have to do with etiquette?" The dictionary defines etiquette as "any special code of behavior or courtesy." Etiquette means knowing what to do when. It also means, as the word "courtesy" implies, treating others kindly. When someone has good manners, they are living the golden rule: Do unto others as you would have them do unto you. If you know the "special code of behavior," then you will know what to do when you are introduced to one of your parents' friends. You will know what to do when you drop a fork in a fine restaurant. You will know what to do about tipping the waiter when you are having lunch with friends.

When you know what to do, you feel comfortable and self-confident, and you enjoy things more. Because you won't be worried about what you are supposed to do, you can put others at ease and make *them* feel more comfortable, too.

Being kind and courteous to others—having good manners—

not only makes you more comfortable; it makes you more popular! And who doesn't wish to be more popular at a time when they feel anything but confident, comfortable, and secure? It is important for you to remember that most people your age have feelings of insecurity. It's normal to have those feelings, but it's also possible to overcome them.

Our hope is that, through the information and situations presented in this book, you will understand that it's possible to feel comfortable in previously uncomfortable situations. You will find that you enjoy being around others more, and that they enjoy being around you.

A Word from the Authors

I wish to dedicate my work on this book to my grandchildren, Casey, Jeep, Paul, Peter, Danny, Willy, Anna, and Liz, some of whom are, and some of whom will be, old enough to enjoy it and benefit from it.

Elizabeth L. Post

My work on this book would not have been possible without the help and guidance of many important people, but most especially my family: Lillian and A. B. Myers, my parents, who instilled important values and codes of conduct that have served me well; Ashley and Preston, my children, who endured, and then politely ignored, my numerous etiquette lectures, but who also provided inspiration and encouragement along the way; Chet, my husband, who loves me—and who *always* encourages me, even though it is *not* always to his advantage to do so!

Joan M. Coles

1

Introductions and Conversations

The impression you make the first time you meet someone is truly important. If the person likes you, you may become friends. If you never see the person again, they'll always remember you as you were the first time they met you.

An important part of any first impression is an attractive appearance. Being pleasant to look at shows that you are considerate of others, and it affects many areas of your life: making friends at school, keeping peace in your family, getting the attention of that special boy or girl, making an impression on a job interview! Remember, you don't want to look at anyone who has tangled hair and a dirty T-shirt any more than they want to look at you that way. If someone doesn't like the way you look (or smell!), they'll probably never get to know you well enough to learn that you can pass a football like a pro, or that you can play all the latest rock hits on your electronic keyboard.

The dream of most kids your age is to be popular. Look at the kids who are well liked. They may not be the prettiest or the most handsome, but they are usually neat, clean, well dressed (not expensive clothes, but clothes that are carefully chosen and well cared for), cheerful, and considerate of others.

People notice how you look when they first meet you, but they also notice what you say and how you act. So, what is the best way to meet or introduce someone . . . and what do you say?

MEETING PEOPLE

When you meet someone for the first time: stand (if you aren't already), smile, look him straight in the eyes (notice we did *not* say look at the floor), extend your right hand and give a firm handshake, then say, "Hello, how are you?" There are certain forms to follow when introducing people, but the most important thing is just to introduce them. Don't be so worried about using the wrong form that you stand there like a dunce and don't make any introductions at all. Just so you'll know how to do it correctly, here are the rules:

- *When introducing boys and girls about the same age,* say the girl's name first: "Susie, this is Freddie Fraternity. Freddie, this is Susie Sorority." Or, even easier: "Susie Sorority, this is Freddie Fraternity."

- *When introducing older and younger people,* say the older person's name first: "Grandma, I'd like you to meet Girla Mydreams. Girla, this is my grandmother, Mrs. Happitameecha."

- *When introducing an important person to someone less important* (and sometimes it's hard to tell which is which), say the important person's name first: "Dr. Stickum, this is Ready Tocry. Ready, this is Dr. Lovesta Stickum."

- *When introducing friends to your parents,* always give your friend's first and last name: "Mom, I'd like you to meet my friend, Penny Perky. Penny, this is my mother." Be sure to add your parent's last name if it is different from yours: "Penny, this is my mother, Mrs. Goodtimes," or "I'd like you to meet my mom and my stepfather, Mr. and Mrs. Fullajoy." Should your mother use a different name than your stepfather, you would say ". . . my mother, Mrs. Goodtimes, and my stepfather, Mr. Fullajoy."

- *When introducing yourself to someone,* just smile, shake his hand, and say, "Hi! My name is Joe Friendly." If he doesn't respond by telling you his name, you may say, "What's your name?" This is a great thing to do when you're at a party where you don't know everyone and the host or hostess doesn't have time to introduce you.

• *When introducing someone to a group,* you say the name of the person being introduced first: "Sally Smiley, these are my friends, Justin Jock, Cathy Coy, and Mary Maker." If you're introducing Sally to a large group, you can say, "Listen, everybody, I want you to meet my friend Sally Smiley. Sally lives in Metro City, and she is spending the weekend with me. Sally, these are my friends . . . " and you can tell her the name of each friend present or you can have your friends introduce themselves.

Points to Remember When Introducing People

Give them something to talk about. When introducing people, tell them a little something about one another. This makes it easier for them to talk if you have to leave them. For instance, "Muffy, this is Henry James Worthalot IV. His hobby is hunting wild animals in Africa. Henry, this is Muffy Spensamore. She runs a wild animal preserve and raises orphaned animals."

What if you've forgotten a name? Don't worry about it. It happens to everyone. You can be direct and say, "I'm sorry. I know we've met, but I don't remember your name." Or if you think they may have also forgotten your name, you can say "Hi. My name is Sam Spaced. I'm sorry I don't remember your name." You may also use the avoidance approach, which is not as good as the direct approach but can sometimes get you out of a tight spot. When introducing someone you know to someone whose name you don't remember, you simply say to the person whose name you don't remember: "Do you know my friend, Ada Glance?" You then pause and hope he'll reply, "No, I don't think so. It's nice to meet you Ada. My name is Don Debonair." If he doesn't catch on and introduce himself, then you just continue talking and Ada may never find out Don's name!

TALKING TO OTHERS

Talking to people you've just met, or to people you don't know very well, is sometimes difficult. Remember these points:

- *Ask questions that don't have yes or no answers.* Instead of saying, "Do you have any plans for the summer?" say, "Tell me about your plans for the summer."

- *Listen to what the other person is saying,* so you'll learn something about him or her. For example:

  Tom: Harry, what are your plans for the summer?
  Harry: I'm going to be working for my father.
  Tom: Really? What does your father do?
  Harry: He owns a computer store and he's going to let me demonstrate the computer games to customers. His partner's daughter is also going to work in the store this summer and boy, is she a knockout.

  Good questions lead to more questions and the conversation can go on forever—much better than those long awkward silences.

- *Be careful when telling jokes.* Ethnic jokes can really offend others. As for "dirty" jokes, you'll probably tell or at least listen to some of them, but try not to use four-letter words. The line between what is funny and what is in bad taste is often hard to draw. When in doubt, steer clear of questionable jokes.

- *Some things are better left unsaid.* Gossip may seem to be a great way to fill the gap in a conversation, but you will find yourself losing friends if you talk badly about them behind their backs. It's okay to say: "Have you heard the good news? Jonathan asked Kristin to go steady." It's not okay to say: "Did you hear about Jonathan and Kristin? They broke up because Kristin found out that Jonathan was dating her best friend while she was out of town." (This example is even more vicious if it's untrue.)

- *Use thoughtful words:*

  "Please," when you're asking for something.
  "Thank you," when you get it.
  "Excuse me," when you've interrupted.
  "I'm sorry," when you've offended.
  "No," when asked to do something that you know is wrong or that you really don't want to do.

- *Listen to yourself.* Do you whine? Do you use the same words over and over—too much slang, y'know? Do you use swear words? Do you grunt instead of saying yes or no? It's possible to correct these habits with a little effort on your part.

- *Know when to make contact and when not to:*

It's Okay	*It's Not Okay*
to speak to a fellow passenger if they want to talk	to initiate a conversation if your fellow passenger is reading or sleeping
to smile at a passing stranger on the street	to go anywhere alone with a stranger or someone you've just met
to talk to your dance partner when dancing, if you want to	to talk to a friend who is working if, by talking to you, he is not doing his or her job
to talk to someone at school that you don't know	to go somewhere with someone you just met at school, until you know them better

To sum up our advice: THINK BEFORE YOU SPEAK! (This goes for telephone conversations, too. See the next chapter.)

2

Telephone Manners

You will probably never again spend as much time on the telephone as you will during your teenage years. If you're going to spend that much time doing something, you might as well learn to do it right! The telephone is not a toy. As much fun as it is to use, it is important that it not be abused. Learning to be courteous and considerate on the phone is a skill that will always serve you well—both in business and in your personal life.

MAKING PHONE CALLS

Always identify yourself, even when you call your best friend. When calling someone you don't know, or who doesn't know you, give your first and last name and any other identifying information.

NOT THIS:

Mark: Hi, Mrs. Neighbor. Do you know who this is?
Mrs. Neighbor: No, I don't know and I don't care. Goodbye.

THIS:

Mark: Mrs. Neighbor, this is Mark Green. My brother, Lon, mowed your lawn before he went away to college.
Mrs. Neighbor: Oh yes, Mark. How are you?
Mark: Fine, thank you. I'll be mowing yards this summer to earn extra money and I would like to mow yours. Could we set up a time to talk about it?

Mrs. Neighbor: Sure, Mark. I'm so glad you called. Could you come by after school on Wednesday?
Mark: Yes, ma'am. I'll be there at 4:00. Thank you.
Mrs. Neighbor: You're welcome, Mark. Goodbye.

If you dial a wrong number, check the number with the person who answers the phone and apologize for disturbing them.

NOT THIS:

Receiver: Hello.
Caller: Oh @#*! [and hangs up].

The caller still doesn't know whether he dialed incorrectly or copied the number incorrectly. He may have disturbed someone who was ill or elderly or in the shower. It's important to have the right number and to dial it carefully.

THIS:

Receiver: Hello.
Caller: Hello, I'm calling the Sports Shack. Is this 342-4709?
Receiver: No, it isn't. This is the Chicken Shack.
Caller: I'm sorry I disturbed you. Goodbye.

The caller then checks his number before he redials.

If you need to talk a long time, ask if it is a convenient time to talk.

NOT THIS:

Sharon: Marsha, IFinishedTheFirstFiveHundredPagesOfMyBook AndIWantToReadThemToYouBecauseYouKnowHowMuchYour OpinionMeansToMe:TheHistoryOfTheWorld—OnceUponATime WhenDinosaursRoamedTheEarth . . .

THIS:

Sharon: Marsha, I want to read you the first five hundred pages of my book. Do you have a couple of hours?
Marsha: No, Sharon, this is not a good time for me. May I call you back next week?

If you must use a business phone, make sure the call is related to that business. If not, use the pay phone.

NOT THIS:

Tami (using the phone at the cosmetics counter): Barbi, this is Tami. I'm so upset. I just saw Sean in the mall. He looked right at me and didn't even speak. I'm devastated! I don't think I can face him in history class tomorrow. I'm just crazy about him and he doesn't even know I exist. Oh, Barbi, what can I do? [This conversation could go on for another hour and a half. It should not take place on a business phone.]

THIS:

Tami (using the phone at the lingerie counter):   Barbi, this is Tami. I'm at the mall and I found the pink and purple polka dot bikini panties you've been looking for. Do you want me to buy them?

Barbi: Oh, Tami, I'm so excited! Please get them for me and I'll pay you back. Thanks bunches!

Tami: You're welcome. I'll bring them to you on my way home. Bye! [Tami then turns to the salesclerk and says, "Thank you for letting me use your phone. My friend would like me to get these panties for her."]

DURING PHONE CONVERSATIONS

Always sound interested in what the caller has to say.

Caller: John, this is Brutus. I broke my knee at football practice today.

John: Uh-huh.

Brutus: I have to stay in the hospital for six months with my leg in traction.

John: Uh-huh [screaming at the TV, "You stupid idiot. Why did you fumble the ball on the one yard line?"].

Brutus: The doctors say I'll never be able to play football again.

John: Well, okay. This is the last ten seconds of the game and I don't want to miss the end. Nice talking to you, Brutus. Goodbye.

Surely you would never be as insensitive as John was to Brutus—would you?

Excuse yourself before talking to someone in the room while you are talking on the phone. It's really annoying to the caller if you don't.

NOT THIS:

Nancy: So Johnny passed me this note in class that said—

Janie (yelling at her little brother):   Get out of my room, stupid!

THIS:

Nancy: So Johnny passed me this note in class that said—

Janie: Excuse me, Nancy, I'm dying to hear what the note said but I need to speak to my brother for a minute. [Then she says to her brother in a normal tone of voice, "Get out of here you little creep, or I'll beat you to a pulp when I get off this phone."] Okay, Nancy, tell me about the note.

Certainly, you would *never* speak to your brother or sister like that, but it was important to illustrate the point.

Never eat while you are talking on the phone. You may drink, if you do it quietly, while the other person is talking. Imagine this scene:

Missy: Hello [munch, crunch].

Topsy: Hi, Missy. This is Topsy. I just had to talk to someone. I started a new diet today and I'm starving.

Missy: Oh you poor thing [crunch, munch, slurp, slurp].

Topsy: All I've had to eat today is one M & M. I think I'm going to pass out!

Missy: [Slurp, belch] Oh Topsy, you can do it. Dieting is easy [crunch, munch, munch, munch]. Look how thin I am [munch, crunch, slurp].

Topsy: Missy, you're no help! I'm going to hang up and fix myself a double chocolate fudge sundae. Goodbye!

RECEIVING PHONE CALLS

If it is inconvenient to talk, for whatever reason (perhaps your family is having dinner, or you have company), ask if you can call back. Quickly explain why you can't talk and must return the call later: "Freddie, I'm dying to talk to you, but we're just having my mother's wonderful chocolate mousse for dessert and I don't want my mousse to melt. May I call you back when I've finished eating?"

If you have a "call waiting" feature on your phone and it is signaling, excuse yourself from the first caller, tell the second caller you'll call back, and go back to the first caller immediately. This is your chance to pretend that you are the busy president of a major corporation. Just say to the second caller, "I'm sorry, Mr. Bigshot, I have someone on the other line. May I call you back in a few minutes?" Sounds pretty good, doesn't it? (Just be sure you remember to call him back!)

When the call is for someone else, put down the phone and go get them. Don't yell!

NOT THIS:

Caller: Hello, this is Tony. May I please speak to Maria?

Maria's brother (yelling): Hey, Maria! It's that creep, Tony. You want me to tell him you're not here?

THIS:

Receiver (cheerfully, of course): Hello.

Caller: This is the President calling. May I please speak to your father? [It is doubtful that the President would make his own phone calls, but it never hurts to be prepared.]

Receiver: Yes, Mr. President, one moment please. [You go get your father and tell him he has a phone call. You do not stand at the phone and yell "Da-a-a-a-ad!"]

When the phone call is for someone who isn't available, offer to take a message or ask if someone else could help them.

Caller: This is Prince Charming. May I please speak to Cinderella?

Receiver: I'm sorry, she isn't here. This is her Fairy Godmother. May I take a message, or would you like to speak to her wicked stepmother?

Caller: You may give her a message. Tell her that I have her glass slipper. I'll call later to see what time I can come by to give it to her.

If you take a message, be sure you have the information correct.

Receiver: Let me check that information, Miss. Your name is Mimi Wannasnowski, and you are calling to tell my mom that the ski lift is broken today. You want her to call you back on Mount Everest at 123-454-3210? I'll give her the message.

If you are leaving a message for someone else, be sure you spell your name and give your number slowly. If possible, tell why you are calling, just as Mimi did.

Telephone Do's and Don'ts

- *DO answer the phone with a smile.* The caller can tell if you are angry or tired or upset.

- *DO keep a list of frequently called numbers near the phone.* Don't try to guess the number or call from memory. Does this sound familiar?

  Caller: Who is this—Betty? I was trying to call Mary Lou.
  Betty: I'm afraid you dialed the wrong number, Clayton. [And you can bet the news will be all over school tomorrow that Clayton has a crush on Mary Lou.]

- *DO have a central family message area,* someplace where everyone knows to check for notes or phone messages—a bulletin board, the refrigerator door, or the television screen.

- *DO negotiate call times with your family,* or ask their permission if you think you'll be on the phone for a while. Your parents will really appreciate it if you say, "Mom, is it okay if I use the phone for a while? I need to call all the cheerleaders and tell them that practice has been changed from Monday to Wednesday." Your mom will be so impressed with your consideration that she won't realize you'll be on the phone for three hours! If she's expecting a call, and she tells you that, then you can complete the calls in about fifteen minutes.

- *DO tape police, fire, ambulance, and local poison control center numbers on the phone.* They're hard to remember in an emergency. Trying to look up the number for the fire department when the ceiling is about to cave in is pretty dangerous; so if you suspect fire, go next door to call. If you think you hear an intruder, lock yourself in a room with a telephone, call the police, and stay there until they arrive.

- *DON'T make any personal telephone calls when you're working or babysitting.* You are being paid to do a job, and you can't do it if you're talking on the phone. Besides, what if the Joneses forgot to tell you that their friend was going to come by and borrow their sports car for the evening? If they couldn't reach you because you were on the phone, you'd spend a few nervous hours worrying about how you were going to explain that somebody stole their car while you were talking on the phone!

- *DON'T place a call after 10 p.m.,* unless you know for sure that *everyone* at the home of the person you're calling is awake. The girl of your dreams may be dreamier than you expected if you call her at midnight!

What About Girls Calling Boys?

In our opinion there are only a few occasions when this is appropriate:

- When you have a question about the frog you dissected in biology class today and your partner was a boy.

- When you are responding to an invitation: "I'd love to go fishing with you and your family next Saturday morning at four a.m. What do I wear?"

- When you are returning a call: "This is Juliet. I'm returning Romeo's call."

- When plans change: "Billy, I can't go fishing with you next Saturday after all. I just got back from the allergist and found out I'm allergic to worms. Thank you for inviting me, though."

- When issuing an invitation: "Paul, I'm having the football team and the pep squad over for pizza after the game on Saturday. Can you come?"

Some of you may not care what our opinion is on the subject of girls calling boys, and may choose to ignore our list of acceptable occasions. If you persist in calling boys for other reasons, please remember that you will make the best impression if you identify yourself when you call (even if your true love's mother answers the phone).

NOT THIS:

Bif's mother: Hello.

Muffy: Oh no! It's his mother. [There are lots of giggles from the background and Muffy hangs up. Mrs. Van Buren demands that Bif pass the word at school that if his mother ever finds out who the girl was who behaved in such an inconsiderate manner, she will call the girl's parents and inform them of their daughter's thoughtless behavior.]

THIS:

Muffy: Mrs. Van Buren, this is Muffy Worthington. May I please speak to Bif?

Mrs. Van Buren: Certainly, Muffy. One moment, please. [Mrs. Van Buren turns to Bif and says, "Muffy Worthington wants to speak to you. She sounds cute!"]

Which reaction would you want from your boyfriend's mother?

What To Do When:

- *You're home alone, and you get a call from someone you don't know.* Do *not* tell them your name or let them know you're alone.

NOT THIS:

Receiver: Hello.
Caller: Who's this?
Receiver: Jimmy Jones.
Caller: Jimmy, may I speak to your mom or dad?
Receiver: They're not here right now. May I take a message?
Caller: No, that's okay.

The caller doesn't need to leave a message. He just found out your name and that you were home alone. If he's a bad guy, you could be in trouble.

THIS:

Receiver: Hello.
Caller: Who's this?
Receiver: Whom do you wish to speak to?
Caller: Your mom or dad. Are they home?
Receiver (this is where you have to tell a little white lie): My dad is, but he's working in the yard right now [or in the shower, or napping]. May I take a message and have him call you back later?
Caller: No, that's okay. Goodbye.

If the caller agrees to leave a message, then he probably is a friend of your parents. You should take his name and number and give it to your parents immediately. You should always know how to call your mom or dad when they're not home (they should leave you a phone number).

- *You receive an obscene telephone call.* If you answer the phone and someone says something that scares you or that you don't understand, do not talk—hang up immediately. Be sure to tell your parents about the call. If such calls persist, they should be reported to the telephone company, and you should follow any recommendations they make. Blowing a whistle into the phone is often a very effective way of deterring such calls.

- *You need emergency assistance.* Stay as calm as possible and give your name, address, telephone number, and describe the problem you are having.

NOT THIS:

Caller: Hello, police? Help! Someone is breaking into my house [and the caller hangs up]!

THIS:

Caller: Hello, police? My name is Rosie Richgirl. Someone is trying to break into my house and steal all my designer clothes. I live at 128 Park Place Drive and my phone number is 123-4567. Please come quickly!

3

Correspondence

Before you learn *what* to say in cards and letters that you send to others, it is important to learn *how* to say it.

BEGINNINGS AND ENDINGS

You begin by deciding what kind of paper you are going to use. There are different types of stationery for different types of correspondence. Personal letters to close friends and family can be written on decorative, colorful, or "fun" paper. Business letters, which may be written to inquire about a job (see page 134) or to purchase or return merchandise, should be written on paper of conservative color with minimal decoration. For long letters, use letter-size stationery with second sheets. For short correspondence, use a card or fold-over note.

Once you get past the third grade, you should write with a pen instead of a pencil! If you have trouble writing without making too many mistakes (lots of people do), make a scratch copy before using your good paper.

Personal letters are handwritten unless your handwriting is hard to read. It's preferable to type business letters, but whether the letter is typewritten or not, *always* sign your name by hand.

Once the pen and paper are ready, you write the date at the upper right side of the page. On personal letters, all you need to write is "Wednesday" or "September 1." On business letters, write the complete date: "September 1, 1990."

It's not necessary to write out your address if you're using a plain sheet of paper. But if you want to, it goes in the upper right-hand corner just above the date, or both the address and date may go in the lower left corner of the page.

You begin your letter with, "Dear ——." How you end it depends on to whom you've written. "Sincerely" is always correct for business letters or letters to mere acquaintances. "Love," "Fondly," or "Affectionately" is correct for friends and relatives. You can also close a letter to a good friend with a phrase such as "Hoping to see you next week," or "Miss you a lot," or just "Always."

Correct forms of address are as follows:

	Address	*Opening of Letter*
Boys under 7	Master Prentiss Cutshaw	Dear Prentiss,
Boys 7 to 18	Jason Morphew	Dear Jason,
Man 18 or over	Mr. Peter Myers	Dear Peter, or Dear Mr. Myers,
Unmarried girl	Miss Sarah Ligon	Dear Sarah, or Dear Miss Ligon,
Woman (marital status unknown)	Ms. Barbara Smart	Dear Ms. Smart,
Married woman	Mrs. J. Clayton Johnson	Dear Mrs. Johnson,
Divorced woman	Mrs. Kathy Waters	Dear Mrs. Waters,
Widowed woman	Mrs. Roy Hanson	Dear Mrs. Hanson,

WRITING THE LETTER (OR, WHAT TO SAY BESIDES "HOW ARE YOU? I AM FINE")

What you say after "Dear" depends on the age and marital status of the person you are writing to, and on how well you know the person. The personal letters that are the most fun to read are those written as if the writer were talking to you. Underline words, capitalize them, use exclamation marks, dashes, and contractions. Which sounds better to you?

Janet and I went to a movie last night. There were some really cute boys sitting on our row.

or

Jan and I went to a movie last night—you should've seen these *fantastic* looking guys sitting on our row!

After you've written the latest news about yourself, ask some questions that your friend can answer when he or she writes back.

Business letters, on the other hand, should get straight to the point and specify what action needs to be taken. For example:

Dear Mail Order Company,

On April 27th I ordered a blue t-shirt from your mail order catalog. When my order was delivered on May 15th it contained a green t-shirt, which I am returning. Please send the blue t-shirt, size medium, if it is still available. If not, please send me a refund.

Thank you,
E. Z. Tapleez

ADDRESSING THE ENVELOPE

When you've written your message, fold the paper to fit the envelope—usually in thirds for letter-size paper and in half for note or small letter paper. Place the paper in the envelope so that when it is removed and opened, it is right side up for the reader.

Your envelope should have a return address (full name, full street address, city, state, and zip code) in the upper left corner,

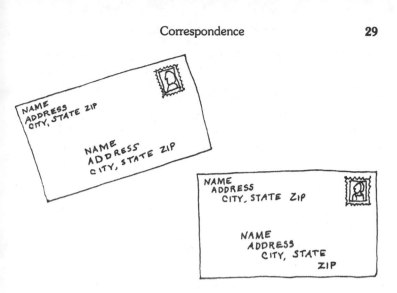

and a stamp in the upper right corner. The mailing address is centered on the face of the envelope, with the second and third lines aligned or indented.

THANK-YOU NOTES

There are many different types of notes and letters, but this is the only kind that *must* be written. Thank-you notes may be written on your personal stationery or on a fold-over note. Printed thank-you cards are unacceptable unless you add a personal note; otherwise they show no real appreciation. Just two or three lines is enough, but it must be personal and it must sound as if you really mean it.

Points to Remember for Writing Thank-You Notes

- Write the note promptly after the event or receipt of the gift— preferably within a week, but better late than never!
- Make it sound friendly and sincere: "I just love the sweater you sent for my birthday—you must have known blue was my favorite color" is better than "Thank you so much for the blue sweater you sent for my birthday."

- Always mention anything that was special about the gift or event: "I loved spending the Easter holidays with you and your family in Florida. I'll never forget flounder fishing by flashlight and our bonfire on the beach."
- Never mention anything that was wrong with the gift or event: "How thoughtful of you to make homemade fudge for my birthday. Our whole family enjoyed it." Not: "My family said the homemade fudge you sent for my birthday was delicious. I didn't get to eat any because I'm allergic to chocolate."
- It's not necessary to write a note for something you have already thanked the giver for enthusiastically in person (unless your parents say you should), but a note is always appreciated. *Exception:* When you have been someone's houseguest, you must write them a note when you return home, no matter how profusely you thanked them when you left!
- When acknowledging a gift of money, give some idea of what you plan to do with it: "The fifty dollars you sent for Christmas will really help me get the ten-speed bike I'm saving for" is better than "I put the fifty dollars you gave me in my bank. I know it will come in handy someday."

NOT THIS:

Dear Susan,
    Thank you so much for the surprise slumber party you gave for my birthday. I was really surprised and had so much fun. You are a good friend.

                                    Sincerely,
                                    Jane Doe

THIS:

Dear Susan,
    I don't think I'll ever forget how surprised I was when I walked into your house and everybody yelled "HAPPY BIRTHDAY!" I know I've never had more fun at a slumber party—and I'm sure this will be my best birthday ever. You are a *wonderful* friend.

                                    Love,
                                    Janie

LETTERS OF APOLOGY

Every once in a while something unfortunate happens for which you must apologize. Sometimes it's easier to write a letter than it is to telephone or make the apology face to face, and sometimes the formality of a letter helps the situation. Here are two examples:

Dear Stewart,

I want to apologize again for letting you know so late last week that I couldn't come to your party on Saturday. I simply had the date of our family vacation mixed up and thought we weren't leaving until Sunday. You always give great parties, so I know I missed a good time! I do hope my absence was not an inconvenience.

Fondly,
Charlotte

Dear Mrs. Harper,

I want to apologize for the carelessness of one of my guests who parked on your lawn during my party last weekend. I have no idea whose car was involved, but please have the damage repaired and send the bill to me.

I will see that my friends are more careful in the future, and I am very sorry that it happened.

Sincerely,
Jack Goodman

SYMPATHY NOTES

It seems that sympathy letters are always difficult to write, whether you knew the person well or hardly at all; but there are times when they are necessary. A handwritten note is always preferable to a purchased greeting card, but it need not be long. If possible, include some little story or something happy you remember about the person who died.

Dear Mr. and Mrs. Jackson,

I was so shocked to hear of John's sudden death. We didn't see each other much except during football season, but I'll never forget the time he recovered the ball that I fumbled on the five yard line. He really saved my skin!

John always kept the team's spirits up when we thought we were losing the game. We'll all miss him.

I know this is a terrible time for you, but please let me know if there is anything I can do.

Very sincerely,
Tommy Thomas

Dear Jenny,

I was really sorry to hear of the death of your grandmother. I used to love to hear you tell about your travels with her. My favorite story was about the time you were in Paris and she ordered the dinner in French—then neither of you had any idea what you were eating! I would have loved to have met her.

I know you'll miss her. My grandmother died two years ago and I still think of her often. Please know that you are in my thoughts and prayers, and let me know if there is anything at all that I can do.

Fondly,
Carolyn

If a close member of your family dies, you may need to help acknowledge flowers, gifts, and written letters of condolence; printed sympathy cards do not require an answer. The funeral home may provide you with printed acknowledgment cards, but they should not be used without the addition of a short handwritten note.

In response to written letters to you, you might say:

Dear Joanne,

Your letter arrived at a time when I really needed the support of my friends. It is a great comfort to know how many people loved Dad, and I want to thank you for writing.

Much love,
Linda

When you're writing the letter for your mother or father, the wording is a little different.

Dear Mrs. Howard,
   Mother has asked me to write and tell you how grateful she was for your sweet letter. I would like to add my thanks to you for writing—notes like yours have been such a great help to all of us at this time.

Sincerely,
Marie Faulkner

LOVE LETTERS

Don't ever write a letter that would embarrass you should it fall into the wrong hands. Of course you always hope that won't happen, but it never hurts to plan ahead. Your boyfriend's mother won't be nearly as upset to read "Skating on the lake last Saturday was so much fun   I hope we get a chance to do it again before spring" as she would be to read "Remember what we did at the lake last Saturday? I hope we get a chance to do it again before spring."

If in doubt about how your letter might sound, keep it over-night and read it once more before you mail it. What you wrote in a moment of anger, boredom, or loneliness may sound pretty silly the morning after!

GREETING CARDS

It's possible to find a greeting card to say just about anything you want to say, but "This reminded me of you" or "With much love" before you sign your name adds a personal touch. This is especially true of Christmas cards; only businesses should send cards with printed names and no handwritten message or signature.

CALLING CARDS

Originally used when paying formal calls on friends, calling cards are now used almost exclusively for enclosures with gifts and flowers. They may be engraved with your full name (shown actual size):

Miss Cynthia Goody Twoshoes

or

John Allen Gotrocks

Or children and young teens may choose a decorated card printed in colored ink and using only their first and last names: Johnny Gotrocks or Cindy Twoshoes.

Whenever you use your card as a gift enclosure, it's nice to write some appropriate greeting such as "Happy Birthday" or "Congratulations," and you may also sign your name.

INVITATIONS

Everyone loves to receive invitations and it's important to let the host know how you feel—that you're excited about attending, or that you're really sorry you won't be able to. (Information about sending invitations can be found on pages 100–101.)

If an invitation does not say "R.s.v.p." (which is French for "Répondez, s'il vous plaît" or "Respond, if you please"), then it is not necessary for you to let the host know whether or not you will attend. If the invitation does say "R.s.v.p." or "Regrets only" or "Please respond" or includes a response card, then you must respond.

Most invitations you receive will be informal; they will be fill-in, preprinted invitations or casually worded printed ones. If "R.s.v.p." is followed by a phone number, then you simply call and let the host know whether or not you'll attend. If "R.s.v.p." is followed by an address, then a short note to the host, such as

"Looking forward to your football party Saturday night," is sufficient. Be sure you respond promptly. Letting the host know you'll attend the day before the party really doesn't help him or her figure out how much food to prepare!

Occasionally you will receive a formal invitation, one that is engraved or handwritten, in the third person, on white or cream cards. As with informal invitations, your response should "match" the invitation. Your formal response should be written in the third person following the correct form. An invitation to a debutante dance might read:

Mr. and Mrs. Rich Worthington
Miss Vera Worthington
request the pleasure of your company
on Friday, the fifth of February
at half after eight o'clock
The Tuxedo Club
Tuxedo Park, New York

R.s.v.p.
18 Park Place   *Dancing*
New York, New York 10001

Your acceptance would read:

Miss Sue Unworthy
accepts with pleasure
the kind invitation of
Mr. and Mrs. Worthington and
Miss Worthington
for Friday, the fifth of February
at half after eight o'clock

Your regret would be the same, except that where the acceptance says "accepts with pleasure" the regret would say "regrets that she is unable to accept."

Sometimes an invitation includes a response card, which looks like this:

> *Warren Harris*
>
> ☐ accepts
> ☐ regrets
>   Friday, February fifth
>   The Tuxedo Club

or

> M_____
>
>   will ____ attend
>
>   Friday, February fifth

All you must do with a response card is fill in your name, indicate whether you accept or regret, and return it as soon as possible.

4

Your Mealtime Manners

DINING AT HOME

When you say the word "etiquette," the idea that usually comes to mind is table manners. It seems to be the area where most people feel unsure. It is pretty hard not to be a little nervous when you are seated at a table with a service plate (what's that?), a forest of crystal, and more knives, forks, and spoons than you ever knew existed. Fortunately this doesn't happen very often—but the next time it does, you'll know what to do.

Family Service

This is the type of meal service with which you are probably most familiar: the whole family sitting down together for a meal. Family style at your house may be eating a pizza from the box or munching a sandwich in front of the TV. We all eat like this occasionally, maybe often, but it is important that we not let it become a habit. Good table manners should be learned and practiced at home. You may not think so now, but someday when you are president of the company, you'll be glad your mom and dad made you set the table, sit up straight, and use your napkin.

Try to set the table several times a week. It helps you become more comfortable about knowing where the forks, knives, spoons, plates, glasses, and napkins go. It's also important for the family to be together at mealtime; sometimes it's the only chance during the day you all have to be with and talk to one another. Besides, you'd be surprised how much better a take-out hamburger tastes on a plate!

Do you dread setting the table because you think you must put a fork, knife, and spoon at each place for *every* meal? Not so! Find out what the menu is and put *only* the utensils needed for that meal on the table. If you're having sandwiches and chips, you don't need any flatware. If you're having soup and crackers, all you need is a spoon. If you're having roast beef, mashed potatoes, and ice cream, then you'll need a fork, knife, and spoon. Doesn't that make sense? No one wants to wash any more utensils than they have to.

What Goes Where

Forks always go to the left of the plate, with the fork to be used first placed farthest from the plate. Exceptions to this rule are the cocktail fork and the dessert fork. The cocktail fork is placed to the right of the spoons or brought in with the appetizer. The dessert fork may be placed above the dinner plate or brought in with the dessert.

Knives always go on the right, next to the plate, with the sharp edge of the blade facing in (to keep you from cutting yourself when picking up other utensils).

Spoons always go to the right of the knives. The dessert spoon may also be placed above the plate or brought in with dessert.

A *service plate* is seen more often in restaurants than in private homes. You will know it when you see it because it is larger than a dinner plate and is used under the plates for the appetizer, soup, and salad courses. It is removed when the entrée is brought in on the dinner plate.

Glasses are placed a little to the right of the tip of the knife.

The *cup and saucer* are placed to the right of the spoons.

The *salad plate* is placed to the left of the forks *if* the salad is served with the entrée and not as a separate course.

The *bread-and-butter plate* is almost always present at restaurant meals, but at home it is usually used only on formal occasions. It should be placed above and slightly to the left of the forks.

Plates may be filled before they are placed on the table, or the food may be passed in serving dishes after everyone is seated and, if it is customary in your home, grace has been said. Food should be passed from left to right, with each person taking a portion that he thinks he can finish. If he cannot reach an item, he should ask the person nearest to that item to pass it. If it's necessary to pass your plate to the head of the table for a second helping, leave the knife and fork on it, but be sure they are securely placed so they won't fall off.

When everyone is finished, napkins should be neatly placed on the table—unfolded, but not crumpled up on the plate. It's also nice if each person takes his plate to the kitchen. If you *must* leave the table before others are finished, ask to be excused.

Buffet Service

These meals are definitely the easiest to serve, and they are often the easiest to eat. If you are planning your first dinner party, make it a buffet.

There are two different ways to present a buffet:

1. The hostess places the beverage, flatware, plates, napkins, and food on one or two buffet tables. Guests help themselves and find a place to sit and eat—not necessarily at a table! Obviously, this is the easiest method for the hostess. It can be lots of fun if the menu is practical and easy to eat while sitting on the floor, the stairs, the sofa, or the piano bench! If no one takes your plate when you are finished, you should take it to the kitchen.

2. The hostess sets the dining table and perhaps some additional tables with silverware, napkins, placecards (if she wishes), and glasses—everything except the dinner plate and the food. Food is placed on a buffet table or sideboard. Guests serve themselves and put their plates at the place assigned by the hostess. If there are no placecards to indicate assigned seats at the table, the guests should place themselves boy, girl, boy, girl, and leave the ends of the table for the host and hostess. Guests should stand behind their chairs until the hostess is seated. Girls are then seated by the boy on their left. If a girl doesn't have a boy on her left, she should seat herself. (Remember, girls, if given a choice, stand to the right of that boy you've had a crush on for weeks!) This is the most difficult buffet for the hostess because

it requires more advance preparation, but it is the easiest for the guest—no worrying about where to sit, or trying to balance food, beverage, napkin, knife, and fork!

LEAVING THE TABLE

If you are dining with family or close friends, you may ask to be excused when you are finished rather than waiting for the others, but this should be done only when you are pressed for time (you have a big history test tomorrow). You should not ask to be excused to go watch your favorite TV program.

Leaving the table during a meal should not occur unless you are coughing or sneezing uncontrollably or need to blow your nose. Try to use the bathroom before you are seated at the table, or wait until you are through eating. If you must answer the phone during a meal, tell the caller you are eating and ask to call him or her back when you are finished.

Have you seen the apron or pot holders that say "Kiss the cook?" It's not a bad idea, if she's your mom or a relative. If she's a friend or your hostess, a big appreciative "thank you" will do quite nicely.

TABLE SERVICE AND PLACE SETTINGS

To help you better understand place settings and table service, let's have an imaginary five-course meal.

The Appetizer

In restaurants there is often a section labeled "appetizers" on the menu. These are items like shrimp cocktail, oysters, pâté, fruit cocktail, or fruit juice. If you order one, the waiter brings the utensil with which to eat it. If you are served an appetizer at a dinner party, use the outermost utensil that looks correct, or watch the hostess. For shrimp cocktail, you use the cocktail fork. For fruit cocktail you use the teaspoon. If the food appears to require a fork larger than a cocktail fork, you use the fork farthest to the left, on the outside. See how easy this is?

The Soup

The soup course is often the hardest course to eat quietly and neatly. It can be done, though, if you hold your spoon properly—the same way you hold your fork: resting on the second finger of your hand with your thumb on top. Never, never hold it the way you hold your toothbrush! Tilt and move the spoon away from you to fill it with soup. Then lift the spoon to your mouth as you lean from the waist over the bowl. Never hunch over the bowl and lower your mouth to the soup! When the soup reaches your lips, quietly sip it from the side or end of the spoon. It is not necessary, or proper, to put the entire spoon into your mouth, unless it's a chunky soup that can't be sipped.

If the soup is served in a soup cup or a cream soup bowl with handles, it is permissible to pick up the cup and drink the soup from it; but you may also use a spoon. Of course, to get that last tasty drop, you must tilt the bowl slightly away from you

and, moving the spoon away from you, scoop it up. Scooping soup and tilting the bowl away from you prevents soup in the lap!

When you are between sips of soup (this is called resting), you may leave your spoon in the bowl, if it is a large one, or you may rest the spoon on the saucer underneath. If your soup is served in a small cup or bowl, you should rest the spoon on the saucer between sips. When you are finished, the spoon is left in a large bowl or soup plate, or on the saucer beneath a soup cup or small bowl—never in the cup.

Must I remind you that you never blow on your soup? If it's too hot to eat, you may *gently* move your spoon back and forth in the soup to incorporate some air into it and cool it. It's also okay to scoop some soup into your spoon and hold it just over the soup bowl for a moment, while you're talking. Unfortunately, neither of these methods ever seem to work fast enough, but they are the only ones that are acceptable when you're dining out.

Croutons (tiny French-fried cubes of bread) are either floated on the soup when it is served or passed separately in a dish with a small serving spoon so that each person may put a spoonful in his soup. Oyster crackers, as well as any other type of cracker, are put on the bread-and-butter plate, or on the tablecloth, and are dropped two or three pieces at a time into the soup. Larger soda crackers, served with chowders, are broken and then, a few pieces at a time, crumbled up and scattered over the soup.

The Salad

In America, the salad is usually served with, or just before, the main course. In Europe and many other parts of the world, it is served following the main course. Either way is correct, and if your hostess has set the table properly, you can tell by the placement of the salad fork when the salad will be served.

When it is served with the entrée, there is no need for a salad fork; you use the dinner fork. When the salad is served separately from the main course, you use the salad fork and salad knife, if one is provided. It is perfectly all right to cut large pieces of lettuce or vegetables with the edge of your salad fork or with the salad fork and knife. However, you should cut only one piece at a time. Don't make a lovely garden salad look like cole slaw by cutting the entire thing into tiny pieces before you eat the first bite!

If you do use a salad knife, it should rest at the top of the plate, blade facing you, when not in use. When you have finished your salad, both the salad fork and knife should be placed in the five o'clock position.

The Main Course, or Entrée

The meat course is usually the main course, or entrée. Now we're probably getting to the part with which you are the most familiar. Want to guess which knife and fork you use for this course? Right! The big ones!

We really didn't think you'd have any trouble knowing which flatware to use for the meat, but we thought you might need to know the proper way to hold them. When you are cutting (one bite at a time, please), the fork should be in your left hand, tines down, and the knife should be held in your right hand as illustrated.

To cut the meat, pierce your next bite with the fork, then cut with the knife about one-quarter inch from your fork. You have

probably already discovered that you can get into big trouble trying to cut too far away from the fork; the whole piece of meat moves back and forth and may knock other food off your plate! If you cut too big a bite, don't try to put it in your mouth; cut it in half and eat each piece separately.

Once you have the bite on your fork, you may raise it to your mouth, still with the fork tines down, and eat it. This is the Continental or European method. It is not seen often in the United States, but it is perfectly permissible. More commonly, after cutting the meat, the knife is placed at the top of the plate, blade facing toward the center of the plate. The fork is then transferred to the right hand, tines up, and this long-awaited bite is eaten!

Obviously, any vegetables that are served with the meat are eaten with your fork. Should you need help getting them onto the fork, you may hold a piece of bread or your knife down on the plate with your left hand. You then push the vegetable onto your fork.

If bread and butter accompany the main course, the butter should be taken from the butter dish and placed on your bread-and-butter plate (that's the small plate just above your fork). If there is no bread-and-butter plate, the butter should be placed on the edge of your dinner plate. Bread and rolls are broken into two or three pieces. To butter them, hold the pieces close to the plate in your fingers—not flat on the palm of your hand! If you want to sop up your gravy, that's fine, but do it by breaking bite-size pieces of bread into the gravy or sauce and using your fork to eat them.

When you have had enough to eat, place your knife and fork in the five o'clock position as you did when you finished your salad. Do not push the plate away from you and say, "I'm stuffed." Something like "That chicken was delicious" is much more appreciated and less offensive.

If you are left-handed, cutting meat or buttering bread may be a little more confusing for you. If you've learned to do these things as right-handers do, that's great! But if it feels unnatural to you then go ahead and hold the knife in your left hand and fork in your right when cutting, and use your left hand to hold your fork when eating. But please do not reverse the place setting itself or the finished position. They should remain as shown.

The Dessert

When preparing to eat dessert, unlike soup or salad, you do not know what utensil you will use until you see the food. Relax. The dessert service should be placed on the table above the dinner plate or brought in with the dessert. It is seldom placed to the left or right of the dinner plate—although a dessert spoon may be placed beside the knife—so don't worry if you run out of flatware before dessert.

If a finger bowl is to be provided, it will be brought to the table with the dessert plate, fork, and spoon. The finger bowl will be sitting on a doily, which will be sitting on the dessert plate. The dessert fork will be on the left side of the plate and the dessert spoon will be on the right. Remove the dessert fork and place it on the table to the left of the plate. Remove the dessert spoon and place it on the table to the right of the plate. Look familiar? Then pick up the doily and finger bowl and place them above and to the left of the dessert plate. When you have eaten your dessert, dip your fingers, one hand at a time, into the finger bowl and swish them around lightly, then dry them on your napkin. You may also touch a little water to your lips with the tips of your fingers if your lips feel greasy.

Leave your napkin on your lap until the hostess places hers on the table. When she does, pick yours up in the center with your left hand and place it to the left of your plate. Never wad your napkin or place it on a dirty plate!

DINING DO'S

- *DO wait until everyone is present before sitting at the table.* This is a really nice practice to start at home; it keeps the family from finishing the meal before Mom gets to the table. It's also nice for the boys in the family to occasionally pull out the chairs for the girls. Remember, practice makes perfect! You can always pretend that your sister is that great-looking girl in science class whom you've been trying to get up the nerve to ask for a date.

(Continued)

DINING DO'S (Continued)

- *DO put your napkin in your lap as soon as you are seated at the table.* It's the first thing you do, even if you are in a restaurant and haven't ordered yet. If the napkin is small, unfold the whole thing in your lap. Resist the temptation to unfold it by flapping it out to the side of your chair! If the napkin is large, you may leave it folded in half in your lap. The only time a napkin should be tucked under your chin is when you are under three years old!

- *DO try a little bit of everything* when you serve yourself (at a buffet, at a family meal, anytime), unless you know you are allergic to a certain food. If your mom or the hostess has taken the time to prepare it, you owe her the courtesy of tasting it. If it looks questionable, you may ask for a small portion. Otherwise, take a medium-size portion, leaving enough for everyone to have one serving of everything. If there is enough food, you may have seconds (or thirds) of your favorites.

- *DO keep dinner conversation pleasant.* Wait until dinner is over to tell your sister about dissecting the frog!

- *DO take small bites* and try to avoid talking with food in your mouth.

- *DO wait until you have swallowed a bite of food before you take a sip of your beverage.* Bread crumbs don't look so great on the rim of the glass—and neither does lipstick, girls, so blot your lipstick before going out when you know you're attending a dinner party.

- *DO remember your posture at the table.* You probably think we mean "Get your elbows off the table," but we are going to tell you that there are times when it is okay to put your elbows on the table. When you are resting between courses, or when you are leaning across the table to talk to someone, nothing is more natural. There is no doubt that this rule was made by the mother of a teenager who insisted on lounging across his food at mealtime—you know, the old wrap-your-arm-around-the-plate-and-hunch-over-the-sandwich routine. Not a very pretty picture, is it? "But how do I keep the lettuce and tomato from falling into my lap," you say. Since you asked—pull your chair up close enough to the table, about four inches from the edge. Then lean from the waist over the plate while you eat. Anything that drops will fall back on the plate. It's really not so hard!

DINING DON'TS

- *DON'T let your eyes get bigger than your stomach when dining out.* Order what you think you will eat. If you just can't finish, most places are happy to give you a take-home bag. Don't be embarrassed to ask for one—it beats wasting money on uneaten food.

- *DON'T use serving utensils for yourself.* Use the sugar spoon to put the sugar in your tea. Use *your* iced-tea spoon to stir it. Use the butter knife to put a pat of butter on your plate. Use *your* butter spreader or dinner knife to spread it on the bread.

- *DON'T put more on your fork or spoon than you can eat in one bite.* Yes, that goes for ice cream, too!

- *DON'T make noise!* Any sound, other than a crunchy veggie or an occasional moan of delight, made while chewing is totally unacceptable. If your mouth is closed when you chew, then you won't have this problem.

- *DON'T mix food on the plate.* It may have been fun to mix your peas and mashed potatoes when you were a child, but one does have to make sacrifices as one grows older!

- *DON'T reach across the table or across another person to get something.* If it's out of reach, ask someone to pass it to you.

- *DON'T pick your teeth at the table,* either with your fingers or with a toothpick. If you have ever seen anyone pick his teeth at the table, you will understand the reason for this rule. It is a real problem if you get a piece of lettuce caught in your teeth at the beginning of the meal. Excuse yourself and take care of the problem in the bathroom.

- *DON'T lean back in your chair.* Keep all four legs of the chair on the floor ("four on the floor"). It is really tempting to lean back on two legs; even grown-ups do it sometimes. The only sure cure we know is to fall backward, break the chair, and have your parents deduct the cost of repair from your allowance. Let's hope you don't have to learn the hard way!

- *DON'T flap your elbows* like a bird flapping its wings when you're cutting or eating. Elbows should be kept close to your sides when eating so you don't jab the person sitting next to you. If you are left-handed, ask to be seated at the corner with your left elbow out. It avoids a collision with your right-handed neighbor.

DINING DILEMMAS

When do I start eating?
At a large party you may start eating after three or four guests have been served. The hostess should say, "Please start or your dinner will get cold," but if she forgets, pick up your fork and others will follow suit. In a group of four or six, it is certainly more polite to wait for everyone to be served.

How do I serve myself from a platter or vegetable dish with one big fork and one big spoon?
Lift the food with the spoon and use the fork to steady it. Replace the spoon and fork on the platter side by side, far enough on it so that there is no danger of their toppling off. If the food is something that's served on toast, such as creamed mushrooms, asparagus, or sweetbreads, slide the spoon under the toast and lift the whole portion carefully—even though you may not wish to eat the toast.

Which way do I pass the food?
When eating family style, food is passed from left to right. When you are served by a servant, food will be presented on your left and removed from your right.

What if I drop my spoon on the floor?
When you drop a knife, fork, or other utensil while dining at home, pick it up, set it aside, and ask for another. In a restaurant, leave it on the floor and ask for another.

What if I drop food or spill something on the table?
If you drop a little food (jelly, peas, or a piece of lettuce) on the table while you are eating, scoop it up with your spoon or the edge of your knife and put it on the edge of your plate. If you have a small spill, dab it with a little water to prevent staining and inform the hostess at the end of the meal. If you have a big spill, she'll know about it, so all you can do is

apologize and help clean it up. If you're dining out and accidentally spill your beverage on the table, blot it with your napkin, then tell the waiter so it can be taken care of.

What if I have to blow my nose, or cough, or sneeze at the table?

If you really must blow your nose during a meal, ask to be excused. It is unlikely that you would have a tissue or handkerchief with you anyway, and we know you would never dream of using your napkin!

Turn your head and cover your mouth with your hand or your napkin when you sneeze or cough at the table. If the attack is prolonged, excuse yourself until it is over.

What do I do with seeds, bones, olive pits, etc.?

Small trash that occurs during a meal should be removed from your mouth discreetly with the thumb and index finger and placed on the bread-and-butter plate or the edge of the dinner plate. Larger objects—gristle, larger bones, skin—should be removed with the fork and placed on the edge of the dinner plate.

Where do I put paper packets from crackers, sugar, salt and pepper?

They should be placed in the ashtray, if no one is using it, or under the rim of the service plate, bread-and-butter plate, or saucer.

What should I do when I'm dining at a friend's house and I finish eating before everyone else?

Make polite conversation until others are finished also, then you may offer to help clear the table. If your offer is declined, don't insist (fat chance!). If your offer is accepted, remove dishes from the right side of the diner. You may take two plates at a time, but never, never stack them.

Helpful Hints for Difficult Foods

- *Artichoke* leaves are eaten with the fingers. They are pulled off one at a time, dipped in the sauce, and scraped between the front teeth to remove the edible pulp. The "choke," which remains on the heart when the leaves are gone, is scraped away with your knife and the heart is eaten with your knife and fork.

- *Asparagus* is traditionally eaten with the fingers, but we're against it. The limp, buttery stalk is not very attractive waving in the air, so it should be cut like any other vegetable.

- *Chicken and chop bones* may be picked up only when you're at an informal affair. Do it as neatly as you can after you've cut off as much meat as possible, and wipe your hands and mouth after each bite.

- *Chicken nuggets, fish sticks, and french fries* are finger foods when eaten as a snack or with other finger foods, but should be eaten with a fork when served as part of a main meal which requires the use of a knife and fork.

- *Corn on the cob* is a stickler, and the best you can do is attack it with as little ferocity as possible. Butter and eat only two or three rows at a time so that you don't have the whole greasy ear smearing your hands and face. Use holders in each end if they are provided; otherwise, corn is strictly a finger food.

- *Finger foods*, such as sandwiches and corn on the cob, are obviously eaten with the fingers. Other foods that will hold together well may also be eaten with the fingers: crisp bacon, bite-size portions of baked potato skins, watermelon, and pickles for instance. However, eclairs or napoleons, whose fillings squirt when they're squeezed, as well as cake with soft icing, must be tackled with a fork.

- *Gravy* is served with a spoon or small ladle, not poured from the gravy boat. It is put right over meat and potatoes or rice. Other accompaniments, such as jelly or relish, are placed beside the food they go with.

- *Spaghetti* is an Italian dish and should be eaten as the Italians eat it. A few strands are held against the edge of the plate (or large spoon, if provided) with the end of the fork, which is then twisted to wrap the spaghetti around the tines. When you have a nice neat coil, get as much to your mouth as possible and bite off the trailers. Don't suck up the ends with a loud slurp!

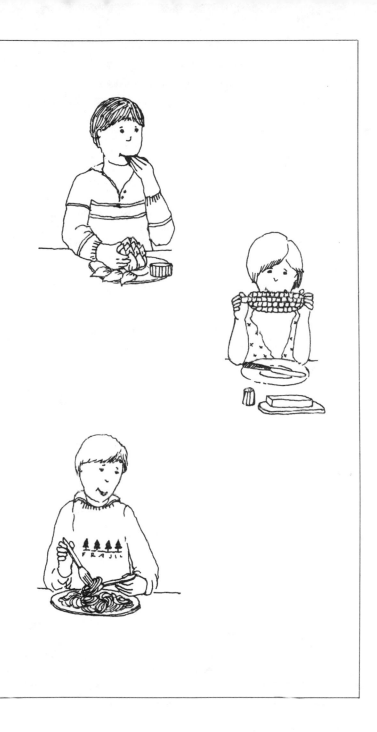

Helpful Hints for Difficult Foods

- *Olives, radishes, and celery* are put on the butter plate if there is one; otherwise they are put on the edge of your dinner plate. They are eaten with the fingers.

- When eating *Oriental food*, forks are usually provided, but don't be afraid to try the chopsticks. They are often presented to you in a paper package as two wooden sticks stuck together, but which are easily separated. Usually the top end is square and the bottom end is round. Use the round end to pick up food and put it in your mouth. The best place to put your fingers is in the middle of the chopsticks. Hold the upper one as you would a pencil—resting on your second finger and supported by your index finger. The upper half of the lower chopstick should rest on the juncture of your thumb and index finger, and the lower half on the end of your ring finger. The lower chopstick stays still and the upper one moves, but to work properly the two ends must be even and not crossed. This does take practice, but it can be great fun to learn with a friend!

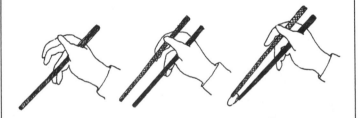

- *Raw fruit* such as apples or pears should be cut into quarters and the core should be removed before the fruit is eaten with the fingers.

- *Shrimp cocktail* is difficult if the shrimp are jumbo size—too big to be eaten in one bite. When they are served in a glass with a stem, knives are not permissible because the glass is apt to tip over. You just have to do your best with the edge of your fork, keeping a firm grip on the shrimp cup with the other hand. When they are served in a stemless bowl or on a plate, you may use your knife to cut them.

RESTAURANT SERVICE

The service in restaurants is as varied as the number of restaurants in existence. They range from fast-food restaurants, where you serve yourself and clean your table, to elegant ones, where silverware is placed according to your order and table service is properly executed.

The important thing to remember about dining in "fancy" restaurants is not to let it make you nervous. Making a mistake is not as disastrous here as it might be at a private dinner party. If you use the wrong fork for your salad, the waiter will either bring you another one or ask you to keep that fork when he removes your plate. Who cares if the waiter knows you made a mistake? It's not the first mistake he's ever seen. There was a time when he didn't know everything, either, and you can be sure there are still some things he doesn't know.

In family restaurants, the utensils which usually appear on the table are the dinner fork, knife, spoon, and sometimes a salad fork. Any other silverware that is required by your order is usually brought to the table at the time the dish is served: (soup comes with the soup spoon, dessert with the dessert, etc.) There is really very little mystery about which utensil to use in a restaurant.

DINING IN PUBLIC

Perhaps you often go to nice restaurants with your family. If so, you're probably very comfortable with the procedure. If not, it's okay because it's not *too* embarrassing to make a mistake in front of your parents. But what about dining out with a friend's family or a date? Are you as comfortable eating out with friends as you are eating out with your family?

To give you an idea of what to expect when dining without your parents, let's run through an imaginary dinner date featuring Jason and Jennifer.

Jason has been dying to ask Jennifer for a date, so he calls her on Wednesday and asks her to go with him to the Snooty Pig restaurant Saturday night. Jennifer is really excited about going to such a special place with Jason; she accepts the date.

Jason then calls the Snooty Pig to make a reservation. The conversation goes something like this:

Snooty Pig: Hello.

Jason: Hello. This is Jason Jones. I'd like to make a reservation for dinner next Saturday, please.

Snooty Pig: Yes, sir. And for what time?

Jason: Seven o'clock, if possible.

Snooty Pig: Fine, how many will be in your party?

Jason: There will be two of us. [Jason may also add that this is a really special date and he'd like a nice table.]

Snooty Pig: Thank you, Mr. Jones. We will look forward to seeing you on Saturday night at seven.

Jason: Thank you. Goodbye.

It's wise to call for reservations several days in advance. Some restaurants do not accept reservations, but it's always good to call and check.

When Jennifer and Jason arrive at the restaurant, Jason lets Jennifer out at the door and goes alone to park the car. Jennifer waits just inside the restaurant door, and they go into the dining room together. If there is a parking attendant (or valet), Jason and Jennifer would both get out at the door and let the valet park the car.

Once inside, Jason checks his coat, but not necessarily Jennifer's. She may, and should, check an umbrella or packages because they are a nuisance at the table, but she ordinarily would wear her coat to the table and drop the shoulders over the back of her chair when she is seated. However, if she is wearing a very bulky down or fur coat, she may ask Jason to check it, too, remembering that he will have to add an additional tip when he retrieves both the coats. (For more information about tipping, see pages 128–30.)

If a headwaiter meets them at the entrance, Jason gives his name and mentions that he has a reservation. Jennifer then follows the headwaiter to their table, with Jason walking behind her. If the table the headwaiter chooses is unacceptable because it's too close to the kitchen or the noisy waiters' station, it's okay to ask for a better one. Jennifer is then given the choice seat—the one with the best view or the comfortable banquette against the wall. When they are both to sit on the

---

Something to Remember About Waiters and Waitresses

There are some very good ones and some very bad ones. The better ones are usually found in better restaurants. It is important that you remember that the waiter is there to serve you (even though they sometimes act as if they were doing you a big favor). This does *not* mean that you should be rude or discourteous. It does mean that you should allow the waiter to do his job. For example, if you ordered a rare hamburger and you got a well-done one, you should discreetly inform the waiter and have him bring you a rare one. If you drop your fork on the floor, leave it there and ask the waiter to bring you a clean one.

For giving good service, the waiter should receive a tip equal to about 15 percent of the check, before sales tax. You see, helping you *is* part of his job. See pages 128–30 if you're unsure about tipping.

---

banquette, Jennifer waits for the waiter to pull out the table and slides in first. At a regular table, the waiter holds the chair for her, and Jason sits down after she is settled. He may, but need not if it's too awkward, help Jennifer off with her coat.

If the restaurant is the type where you seat yourself, Jason leads the way to a table and pulls out a chair for Jennifer. If he really wants to chalk up some credits, he may ask her, "Do you want to sit by the window, or shall we take that little table in the corner where we can talk?"

Ordering Is Fun!

Jason asks for the menu if it hasn't been handed to them already, and the fun begins. They talk about what looks good, and what they are familiar with. Jennifer asks Jason what he's planning to have. His answer will give her a hint about how much he is able to spend. Unless Jason says, "I'm having the chicken, but you order anything you want," Jennifer should not order anything that costs more than Jason's selection.

In some really fancy restaurants, the woman's menu doesn't have any prices on it. It's preferable for Jennifer to say, "My menu doesn't have any prices on it—help me make a selection." But if she's just too embarrassed to say anything, she can order chicken or pasta instead of steak or veal, because they are usually less expensive, or she can order the same thing Jason does.

When the waiter comes to take their order, Jason and Jennifer ask him to describe the zabaglione, gazpacho, and anything else they have a question about. They may also ask him to describe the soup and vegetables of the day; and if they are having trouble making a decision, they can ask the waiter for his recommendation. They should never be embarrassed to ask questions about the menu. There are usually "specials" for the evening that aren't on the menu. It's the waiter's job to answer questions about the food, and by asking, you make his work more interesting.

Menus

There are two kinds of menus—à la carte and table d'hôte—and you need to know what each means. An à la carte menu lists each item with a price beside it, and the cost of each item you order, including beverages, is added up to make your total bill. Table d'hôte, or "complete dinner," has a price beside the main course (often called the entrée) and then lists certain items—appetizers, soups, vegetables, salads, and desserts—with no prices. You may choose one item from each of these groups, unless the menu says otherwise, and the cost is included in the price of the entrée. However, beware! There are almost always some items listed in these categories which *do* have prices beside them, and if they do, that amount is charged in addition to that of the main course. Many "complete dinner" menus will say "Price of entrée includes vegetable, potatoes, and dessert." That means the price of anything else—soup, salad, coffee—will be added to your bill.

Table d'hôte dinners are usually less expensive than the same items ordered one by one à la carte, but remember that you must stay within the limits of what the menu says or the cost of your dinner goes up!

Once the decisions are made, Jennifer tells Jason what she has decided on, and he gives the order to the waiter. If the waiter comes before she's told Jason her selection, or if he asks her how she wants her steak cooked or what sort of salad dressing she prefers, she answers him directly, not relaying her words through Jason. Jennifer doesn't have to order as many courses as Jason, but she certainly shouldn't order more— especially if she wants Jason to ask her out again!

Enjoying the Dinner

When the waiter brings bread and butter or crackers, Jennifer and Jason should refrain from diving in as if they were on the verge of starvation. Gorging on hot bread and exotic crackers is tempting, but it takes the edge off the appetite for the better things to follow.

Table manners are the same in a restaurant as they are at home. The piece of silver farthest from the plate is the one used first, unless a special implement such as a cocktail fork is brought in with the shrimp or other appetizer. Bread should be broken into reasonable-size (not bite-size) pieces. If necessary, salad may be cut with a knife. Except at a very informal "chicken in the basket" type of restaurant, meat is always cut off the bones, and the bones are not picked up with the fingers. A person on a diet should order only what he or she will eat. It is inconsiderate to send most of the food back to the kitchen uneaten.

If Jason or Jennifer orders something that they have never seen before and neither one knows how it should be eaten, there's no cause for panic. (See "Helpful Hints for Difficult Foods," pages 54–56.) No one else in the restaurant is likely to be paying attention anyway. So as long as Jason goes slowly and doesn't make a mess of the table as he's eating the lobster, for example, and Jennifer doesn't break into hysterical laughter watching him, the difficulty will pass unnoticed. They can ask the waiter how to manage, but if they don't want to do that, they should just attack it in the neatest way they can invent.

Time to Go

After their delightful dinner, Jason asks for the check. While he is going over it mentally, not with a pencil and calculator, Jennifer excuses herself to go to the ladies room. Although she could re-apply her lipstick at the table, she should not comb her hair or do any other makeup repairs there, and Jason will probably appreciate the time to take care of the check.

If Jennifer doesn't know where the ladies room is, she need not hesitate to ask the nearest waiter; he is asked the same question at least a dozen times a night. If there is a rest-room attendant and she provides a service such as a clean towel, hair spray, or hand lotion, there will be a little dish in an obvious place and Jennifer is expected to leave a tip of 50¢, or even $1 in a *very* plush restaurant.

When the waiter returns with the change, Jason picks it up and leaves the tip. Fifteen percent of the bill is still the accepted tip everywhere but in the most luxurious restaurants. To figure it quickly, take 10 percent of the total and add half of that amount (see page 129). If Jason is using a credit card, then the waiter will fill in a subtotal, leaving the space for the tip blank. Jason fills in a figure that is about 15 percent, totals the bill, and signs the check. The waiter will give Jason one copy of the credit slip and keep the rest.

Jason helps Jennifer into her coat, and then holds her chair or pulls the table away so that she can get up easily. They both make sure that they haven't left anything at the table; thank the waiter if he is nearby; and leave. If the check says "Please pay cashier," Jason would leave the correct amount for the tip on the table and he and Jennifer would stop at the cashier's desk to pay the check. If he did not have the correct change for the tip, he would return to leave it on the table after getting change from the cashier. On the way out, they retrieve Jason's coat from the checkroom, and he deposits 50¢ to $1 in the plate.

Special Situations

Jason and Jennifer's dinner was a very easy and pleasant one—nothing horrible or embarrassing happened. And this is the way dining out generally is. Sometimes complications arise, but if you know how to handle any unusual situation, every dinner can go as smoothly as Jennifer and Jason's.

The Polite Protector

There are unfortunate occasions when something does go wrong. You find a fly in your soup or lipstick on the glass, or your rare steak arrives looking like shoe leather. It's the man's job to complain, so if the girl has a problem she lets him take care of it. She stays out of the discussion, and he handles it firmly but quietly. He calls the waiter and asks for another cup of soup or a fresh glass, or explains that he ordered the steak rare and it's well done. If the waiter doesn't cooperate, he catches the headwaiter's eye and explains the situation to him. You may reduce the amount of your tip or leave none at all if the waiter has been really rude, and don't go back to that restaurant. But don't ruin the evening for yourself and your date by causing a scene.

Hi, Hello, and Move Along

If you see a group of friends at a nearby table when you arrive, stop and greet them with a "Hi, we didn't know you were coming here tonight," or some such remark, and move on. When you stop to chat, the boys at the table should all stand, and then you'll be cluttering up the passageway for waiters and other customers. If their table is off to one side, just wave; or the first group to leave might stop at the other's table for a brief "Hello." Save those long conversations for another time. It is inconsiderate of the gentlemen standing and the waiters detouring around you to visit tableside any longer than a half a minute.

Suggestions for Smokers

If one member of a couple smokes and the other doesn't, the smoker should ask permission before lighting up. If your date allows you to smoke, be careful that the smoke from a cigarette left in an ashtray doesn't drift directly into your companion's face or toward your nearby neighbors. Don't exhale the smoke in anyone's face, either; that's very annoying to a non-smoker.

When there is no ashtray on the table, ask for one. It is

disgusting to put out cigarettes or drop ashes on the edge of a plate, in your saucer, or on the floor.

When There's Dancing

When you go to a place where there is dance music, you may get up to dance after you have ordered, while waiting for your meal. Keep an eye on the table, though, so that your soup or meat won't get cold. If the music is so good you can't resist it, dance between courses too, but save a little strength—after dinner you can dance to your heart's content.

Many girls wonder what to do with their purses when they get up to dance. Leave your purse on the chair seat and push the chair well under the table. There are very small evening bags and shoulder bags that can be held in the left hand or worn while dancing, but they may put a crimp in your style!

Tipping Headwaiters

A young man or woman is not expected to tip a headwaiter for simply leading him and his date to a table. A tip is expected if the headwaiter has gone to some trouble to put tables together to accommodate a group, has seen to it than an overdone steak was quickly replaced by a rare one, or has performed any service that could be considered special (see page 129). When a boy or a girl entertains a group at a restaurant, then the headwaiter who takes care of the party is given a tip, usually $5 or more, depending on the amount of service provided.

Going Dutch

One of the bigger dilemmas about going Dutch is figuring out whether or not an invitation *is* Dutch treat. For instance: "Let's meet for a pizza" is not necessarily an offer to pay, but "May I take you out for pizza" probably is. If you're not sure, try to clarify, before accepting, by the least uncomfortable means. Your response to "Would you like to meet me for pizza?" might be a lighthearted "That depends on who's treating," or "I'd love to but I'm short on funds this week—how about a burger instead?" Either response will get you the needed information and is certainly easier than being caught in a situation where you don't have enough money.

Once you and your friend(s) have decided to go Dutch, there are several ways you can handle the check. If the restaurant allows it, each person should order his own meal and get a separate check. Otherwise, appoint one person banker. He can collect more than enough money from everyone before you enter the restaurant, pay the check and tip at the end of the meal, then divide the remainder evenly. Or, if the banker has enough money of his own, he can pay the check and tip (or use a credit card), then have everyone else pay him back. Unless there is a large discrepancy in the amount each person ordered, it's best to divide the check evenly. The one thing to avoid is that confusing and ridiculous situation where each member of the group tries to add up his or her share and argues about whose dinner cost 15¢ more. The waiter goes crazy, the other patrons think you're too young to be out without your parents, and your own party ends up in a royal battle.

Dining Alone

At your age there probably aren't many times when you eat out alone—but sometimes it happens. Often people feel awkward about eating alone, but it really can be very nice. You can order what you want and eat at your own pace . . . no need to speed up or wait for someone else!

Ask for a table that you like, one with a view out the window or off to the side so you can feel less conspicuous. Take along a book or magazine; it's okay to read at the table when you're alone and it helps pass the time between courses. Once you realize that most people are not paying any attention to you or feeling sorry for you, you can really enjoy the time alone.

Foreign Restaurants

When you reach the point where you just cannot look at another burger, try foreign food. Chinese, Japanese, Italian, Mexican, French, German, Lebanese—the list goes on and on. The foods will be as familiar as pizza and tacos or as unfamiliar as escargots and sushi, but don't be afraid to try the unfamiliar ones. Remember, there was a time when you had never had pizza!

Most menus written in a foreign language have English descriptions also. If not, don't be afraid to ask. The more exotic the food, the more accustomed the waiters are to assisting you.

Ask for their specialties and recommendations. You may find that gelato (Italian ice cream) is one of your favorite foods!

French restaurants seem to be the worst about giving English translations on the menu. Here are a few words that it might be helpful to know:

French	English
Apéritif	Appetizer, but sometimes means cocktail
Hors d'oeuvre	Appetizer or first course
Pâté	Paste made of meats, usually liver, and seasonings
Escargots	Snails, cooked in strong garlic butter
Moules	Mussels
Soupe, Potage	Soups
Bisque	Rich soup with shellfish
Bouillabaisse	Fish soup (main course)
Vichyssoise	Cold potato soup
Soupe/Potage du jour	Soup of the day
Oeufs	Eggs
Fromage	Cheese
Poisson	Fish
Coquillages	Shellfish
Viandes	Meats
Ragoût	Stew
Agneau, Mouton	Lamb
Boeuf	Beef
Jambon	Ham
Porc	Pork
Veau	Veal
Foie	Liver
Langue	Tongue
Rognons	Kidneys
Saucisse	Sausage
Voilaille	Fowl
Poulet, Coq	Chicken
Faisan	Pheasant
Canard	Duck
Légumes	Vegetables
Fruits	Fruits
Desserts	Desserts
Pâtisseries	Pastries
Boissons	Beverages
Pain	Bread

5

Family and Home Life

Being a teenager is really confusing! It's confusing to you; it's confusing to your family; and it's confusing to your friends. Behavior that your parents used to excuse because you were young and "didn't know any better" they don't excuse any more because now you're older and "you should know better." When you were younger and your parents' friends came to visit, you could say, "Hello, Mr. and Mrs. Jones," and skip merrily away. Now that you are older, your parents expect you to stand and acknowledge Mr. and Mrs. Jones, shake their hands, and make conversation with them for a few minutes before excusing yourself.

No matter how "out of it" your parents seem to be, remember that they've had lots more experience than you, so you must respect their advice and decisions. On the other hand, your mother and father should realize that, although you do need some supervision, you should also be encouraged to make your own choices.

CONSIDERATION FOR OTHERS

Etiquette is basically unselfishness, kindness, and consideration toward others. It gives you guidelines on how to act in almost every situation involving contact with other people. It provides a bridge between you and your parents, you and your friends, and between your childhood and your adulthood.

Family

Your family and your home are your own little world. Parents'
and siblings' attitudes toward you have a lot to do with how you
feel about yourself. The atmosphere in your home, how people
deal with and feel about one another, has a lot to do with how
you deal with the rest of the world. Therefore, family relationships are very important, as is respect for one another. The manner in which you speak to your parents is important. Call them
"Mom" and "Dad" or whatever derivative of "Mother" and
"Father" you prefer. A stepparent or family friend may ask to
be called by his first name or a special nickname. But you should
avoid calling your parents or any adult a name which could be
considered disrespectful. You should also let your parents know
if you are offended by a name they call you. "Bunnykins" is cute
and affectionate, but "Knucklehead" and "Dumbo" are hurtful.

What if you don't like the way your parents treat you? What
can you do if your siblings act as if they hate you? Look at your
own behavior. How do you treat the rest of your family? Is it
the way you would like *them* to treat *you*?

What do you do when your mom calls you while you're
watching your favorite TV program?

NOT THIS:

Mom: Robert.

Robert: Whu-u-ut? [Usually said with a whine; you might recognize
this sound as a very agitated "What?"]

Mom: Trash pickup is tomorrow. Will you please take the trash cans
out?

Robert: Aw-w-w, Mom. Do I have to do it now? This is my favorite
cartoon show . . . and besides, none of my friends have to take out
the trash at their house.

Mom: I don't care what your friends do. I'm telling you to take out
the trash and I want you to do it now. You're too old to be watching
cartoons anyway. Turn off the TV!

THIS:

Mom: Robert.

Robert (in a friendly tone):   What d'ya need, Mom?

Mom: Trash pickup is tomorrow. Will you take out the trash cans, please?

Robert: Sure, Mom, I'll take them out. Do you mind if I wait until a commercial? I'm watching TV.

Mom: That will be fine. Thanks for the help.

Or how about this situation with your sister:

NOT THIS:

Sis: What color blush is that you're wearing, Jenny?

Jenny (suspiciously): Why do *you* want to know?

Sis: Because it's awful, and I want to know the name of it so I'll never buy that color.

THIS:

Sis: What color blush is that you're wearing, Jenny?

Jenny: I think it's called Ripe Peach. Do you like it?

Sis: I do, but I think I like the tangerine color you wore last week better with your skin tone.

Which example do you think works better? Sometimes the tone of your voice tells people the kind of reaction you expect to get, and they'll usually oblige you. So, expect the best, and most of the time you'll get it!

Of course, there will be times when no matter how hard you try, you don't get what you want. Save your ammunition for important things. If you don't put up an argument or make a crisis out of every adverse decision your parents hand down, they'll be much more willing to listen when you ask calmly, not hysterically, for a really important permission. If your argument is sound, and not based entirely on the fact that "everyone else is doing it," you'll have a much better chance of parental approval.

Remember that your parents are human. The minute your dad gets home from work, or while your mom is trying to get dinner on the table, is not the time to bring up an important or controversial topic. That's much better talked about over dessert.

Frankness and communication are vital to family harmony. If you have something on your mind, speak up! Often your parents are wondering why you've been moping around the house for days . . . and they may be relieved to hear that the only thing bothering you is that you need a raise in your allowance! The reverse is true, also. If your dad has been crabby for the last day or two, ask him if it's something you've done, or failed to do. You may be relieved to hear that his stress has to do with something outside the home—perhaps the loss of an important sale at the office. Airing problems has always been the best way to solve or at least diminish them.

What about brothers and sisters? The fact that siblings live under the same roof and can't avoid each other doesn't mean that they always like each other. Your feelings toward one another may change from day to day. But, however you feel, if you recognize that they are individuals with just as many problems as you have, that their likes and dislikes may not be similar to yours, and that they have the right to share your parents' affections with you, family relations will run much more smoothly.

Harmony on the Home Front

Some of these tips may help you in dealing with your brothers and sisters:

- *Avoid jealousy.* It's not easy when sister Sue has gorgeous blond hair or brother Pete is the star on every team at school. Maybe your parents are even guilty of comparing you to your sibling. Don't make those kinds of comparisons. You're different from your brother or sister, so why shouldn't you look and act differently? Think about your piercing blue eyes, or your ability to play the piano. If you can realize or develop your own assets, you won't be threatened by the looks and actions of others.

- *Respect privacy.* Diaries and letters are personal. They may never be opened or read without the owner's permission—no matter how badly you want to know who your sister's latest crush is. The same goes for telephone calls.

  Privacy is also important when you are entertaining. You don't want your little brother annoying the friends at your slumber party any more than he wants you helping to open the presents at his birthday party. Stay away from your brother's or sister's parties unless you're really urged to be there.

- *Make some private time for yourself.* Everyone needs time alone to think, read, rest, or relax. A closed door requires a knock and a "Come in" before entering, and therefore ensures privacy. A locked door is a "no-no." It implies that you don't trust your family; and it is sometimes dangerous. Suppose you slip in the bathtub and break your leg. Your rescue would definitely be hindered by a locked door!

Use your quiet time wisely. Replenish your energy and renew your spirit—but don't run away from your problems. Closing the door to your room will not shut out your problems.

- *Know when to tell and when not to tell*—but that's easier said than done! *Don't* tell just to get your sibling in trouble, or to make yourself look good. *Do* tell when your brother or sister is doing something that is harmful to them or others, or that is dangerous, or that is against the law.

NOT THIS:

You: Mom, Jeff didn't make his bed this morning.

You: Mom, I took my plate to the kitchen and picked up my place mat and napkin, but Amy left hers on the table.

THIS:

You: Mom, I'm really concerned about Jimmy. He told me he's been drinking with his friends every afternoon after school. You think he's in his room doing his homework when you get home from work, but he's not. He's in his room because he doesn't want you to know he's been drinking.

Mom: I'm so glad you told me about this, Joey. I had no idea. It really shows you care about Jimmy.

Most teens *really* don't like to "tell" on a friend or sibling. The more serious the matter, the harder it seems to tell someone else about it. But what's harder: telling your parents about your brother's drinking problem, or seeing him get killed in an automobile accident while driving drunk?

Guests in Your Home

How do you like to be treated when you visit a friend? Suppose he greets you at the door with an enthusiastic "Hi!" or when you walk into the room where he's watching TV, he says, "Hi, Laura. I just started watching some old *Road Runner* cartoons. Want to watch with me?" Then, of course, you'll feel that your friend is glad to see you. You wouldn't feel very welcome if he just grunted as if to say, "Oh no, not you again."

Guests in your home feel the same way. They want to think you are glad to see them. So stand and greet your parents' friends (enthusiastically!), even though you aren't always too happy to see them. Nothing makes your parents more proud than to have you stand, shake hands, and engage in a few minutes of polite conversation with their friends. Maybe Mrs. Johnson does ask dumb questions like, "How's school?" But maybe that's all she knows about you. Instead of answering "It's okay," say something like, "I don't like some of the classes much, but I'm having a great time playing basketball." You don't have to outline the rules of the game for her—just a minute or two of making her feel that you're glad to see her is all that's necessary. Who knows? Maybe she'll give you her basketball tickets the next time she's unable to attend the game!

Household Help

Anyone working for your family—a housekeeper, cook, gardener, or plumber—deserves to be treated with respect and consideration. Presumably your parents have outlined their duties. You may ask, politely, for an occasional favor such as getting a shirt or blouse ironed, but don't add a lot of extra chores to their regular duties, and don't ever give orders yourself.

Family Possessions

Being considerate of the people in your family also means being considerate about their things. Maybe you don't bother to ask your mom if you can borrow her gloves because you know she'll say yes. But what happens when she's ready to go out shopping and her gloves are in your locker at school? She'll probably spend half an hour looking for them, or maybe even think she's lost them. Is that really fair?

Each family member deserves to have control over his or her own possessions. Your mom will probably let you use her gloves, but she has the right to know where they are. And you have a right to know where your things are. Your sister should not borrow your court shoes for her tennis game any more than you should borrow her racquet without asking.

Having control over your possessions not only means knowing where they are; it also means taking care of them. If you wad your Sunday clothes up and throw them into a corner after church, then whose fault is it when they are not cleaned and pressed for the next Sunday? If it's your responsibility to feed the goldfish every day, then you need to ask someone else to do it while you're away at summer camp, or face the prospect of dead goldfish when you get home!

Televisions and Radios

TV sets and radios are usually community property, so the whole family has to take care of them. Don't fool with a complicated VCR or sound system unless you know how to use it.

Keep the sound at a level that is considerate of other members of the family. You don't want to be wakened from a nap by the opening bars of Beethoven's Fifth any more than your parents wish to be wakened by screeching guitars and vibrating drums! Remember to turn off TVs and radios when they are not in use.

Small radios or tape players with earphones are perfect for keeping the noise level down in the house, but they really can damage your ears if you play them too loudly. You should also keep the volume low enough when biking or jogging to be able to hear approaching cars or warning sounds. Remember, too, that wearing earphones and listening to music in the presence of other people is an indication that you do not desire their company. If that is true, leave the room and listen to your music in private, or ask to be excused from the conversation. Just think how annoyed you'd be if you were trying to tell your mom some really important news while she was wearing earphones and listening to her favorite rock station!

The Family Car

Use of the family car is probably the biggest responsibility a teenager can have. The fact that your mother and father consider you mature enough to have earned the privilege of driving is a real demonstration of their trust in you. Try never to betray that trust.

Remember that a car is an expensive possession, costly both to buy and to maintain. Extra insurance fees will be charged because of your use of the car, and there will be increased cost for gas and maintenance. It would be nice to help pay for some of these expenses with your allowance or extra money that you earn . . . or you may want to trade services, such as car washing or waxing or chauffering your little brother in exchange for a certain number of gallons of gasoline.

You'll be excited about using the car when you first get your license, but remember that the family car does belong to your parents and they have the first right to it. The following pointers will help keep your parents happy and you driving.

- *Ask in advance* for use of the car so your parents can plan accordingly. Take turns double-dating with a friend so you aren't asking for the car *every* weekend.

- *Never take the car without permission.* How are your parents to know it wasn't stolen? Your parents need to know where you are going when they let you use the car.

- *Obey the law.* Speeding or drag racing is very, very dangerous. Driving drunk is no better than murder. It is not only the greatest cause of accidents; it can land you in jail or leave you without a license for the rest of your life. If you do take a drink, even beer, be sure that there is someone with you who does not drink, or call a taxi, to get you home. Even running a stop light can cost you your life. Don't take a chance. It really is better to be safe than sorry.

- *Offer to run errands* before you are asked. You'll pile up lots of credit by taking your little sister to dancing lessons or going—cheerfully—for a forgotten quart of milk.

- *Clean out the car after using it.* Your mom won't think it's funny to sit on a half-eaten chocolate bar in her good dress—I'll bet your date wouldn't think it was too funny, either!

- *Accept "No" gracefully.* There will be times when it is not possible for you to use the family car. Try to understand the reason the permission was denied without stomping your feet and slamming doors. Temper tantrums only make your parents mad, and they rarely get you the results you want.

Family Rooms

Responsibility for shared family rooms lies with the whole family. How do you feel when your friend comes to visit if your sister's underwear is strewn all over the bathroom? Or how does your dad feel when his boss drops by to pick up some papers and trips over your shoes in the front hall? No family member has to be embarrassed by a house that looks as if it had just been declared a national disaster area, if each person does his share of the picking up. Maybe the mess in your room doesn't bother you and you can negotiate the cleaning chores with your parents, but do your very best to keep the family rooms presentable.

After you and your friends have used the family rooms, it is up to you to throw out soft drink containers and potato chip bags, to pick up magazines, cards, and books from the floor, and generally leave the room ready for the next person.

Kitchen rules are up to your mother, but she should not be expected to cope with the aftermath of a teenage refrigerator raid! Check with your mom before consuming something that looks as if it might have been intended for dinner. Rinse and stack your dirty dishes in the sink—or better yet, wash them or put them in the dishwasher. It only takes you a minute or two to take care of your own mess, but it takes your mom hours if she has to clean up after everyone.

Sharing a bathroom can also put a strain on family relations. Finding wet towels on the floor, a ring around the bathtub, and a toothpaste tube that's been squeezed in the middle can be

infuriating! Not to mention when someone hogs use of the bathroom for hours on end. You may need to negotiate bathroom times and clean up. But you'll never go wrong if you leave the bathroom the way you'd like to find it.

WORKING PARENTS

There was a time when almost every family was headed by two adults who were married to each other. The husband and father worked outside the home and the wife and mother stayed home to raise their children. Some families are still like that, but in many others the children live with a single parent, a parent and a stepparent, a relative, or divide their time between parents. Because of these types of living arrangements, and because in many families both parents work, it is often necessary for kids to come home to an empty house or to stay home alone.

Everyone needs a little quiet time sometimes, so look at the positive side. You can use this time for homework, or reading, or a hobby that you enjoy. But maybe you get too much quiet time. If you feel lonely or frightened at times, you may want to call a friend or relative, visit a neighbor (with your parents' permission), or play with your pet.

Here are some guidelines that should be helpful to you when you're alone. Look them over with your parents and discuss them. Together, discuss whether or not you may have friends over, where you may or may not go, and so on. You or your parents may want to add or alter these guidelines. Perhaps your parents want you to call them at work each day when you get home. Maybe you want to make arrangements to go to your grandmother's house once a week. You and your parents will be happier if you work together to make your time alone safer and more enjoyable.

When You're Away from Home

- *Always carry money for a phone call.* If you lose your key or miss your bus, you'll be able to call someone to help you.

- *Hide your key in an unlikely place, take it with you, or leave it with a neighbor.* Hiding it under the doormat, in the mailbox, or on a nail in the garage is too obvious. See if you can think of a place no one would ever think to look, preferably some distance from the door.

- *Choose a code word that your parents will tell to other adults they send to pick you up.* Then, if someone offers you a ride and says your parents sent them, but they don't know the code word, you know not to take the ride. *Never* go anywhere with someone you don't know unless they give you the code word.

When You Return Home

- *Pick up the mail and newspaper.* This indicates to strangers in the neighborhood that someone is home. Open only the mail that is addressed to you and put the rest in the same place every day so that your parents will know where to look for it.

- *Don't go into your house or apartment if something looks suspicious.* If the door is ajar or something looks strange to you, go to a neighbor's house and call your parents for advice. If you're unable to reach them, call the police.

- *Once inside, keep the door locked.* Also, lock it if you leave, even "just for a minute," to play with the dog or a friend.

- *Don't leave home without your parents' permission.* Even if you're just running next door for a minute, let one of your parents know. A short visit could turn into a long one, and your parents will be very worried if they are unable to reach you.

- *Never open the door to strangers.* Get your parents to install a peephole if you don't have one. You must be able to see who is at the door. If it's someone you know (Grandma!), then you may open the door. If it isn't anyone you know, even if they say your parents sent them or they're the plumber or the bug spray man, *don't* let them in. Give them a specific time to come back when you know your parents will be home (Thursday at 6:00). If the person doesn't go away, call the police. Don't feel dumb or rude about not letting someone in. It's better to be safe than sorry.

- *Never take medication when you're home alone* unless your parents instruct you to do so. If you're by yourself and you don't feel well, call one of your parents. Follow their directions. If you get worse, call them again. If you feel so bad that you really don't want to be home alone, tell your parents that also.

- *Keep a list of important telephone numbers near the phone.* These should include your parents' work numbers, relatives' phone numbers, neighbors' phone numbers, emergency, medical, and fire department numbers, as well as the numbers of some of your friends. This list should always be kept in the same place so that you can find it when you need it.

- *Use your time wisely.* Finish your homework before your parents get home. Or help with the chores around the house. Maybe you'll want to start dinner (with your parents' permission to use the stove, of course), or vacuum or dust. You may not especially like doing some of these things, but it will be a great help to your parents and will give them more time to spend with you when they get home.

WHEN THINGS GO WRONG AT HOME

You

How much trouble at home do *you* cause? Do you smile more often than you frown? Are you a good listener? Do you share both your joys and your sorrows with your family? Do you treat other members of the family as you would wish to be treated?

How do you act at home when you are depressed or upset about something? Do you yell at your brothers and sisters for no apparent reason? Do you turn the radio up full blast to drown out your troubles? Do you slam doors and stomp your feet? Do you close yourself in your room, coming out only for meals and phone calls? Do you give your parents the old silent treatment? If so, it's no wonder that your family is impatient with you and makes your life more miserable than it already is. How can they help you or support you if you won't share what's on your mind? There is nothing so awful that it can't be shared with those who love and care about you. The risk is well worth the reward. The next time you feel bad, share it, and see what happens.

Your Family

The two biggest causes of stress for people of any age are change and loss. As a teenager, you are "losing" your childhood and "changing" to an adult; your parents are "losing" a child . . . so even if you don't have any of the big problems mentioned here, you'll have a certain amount of stress that comes from just growing up!

Sometimes there is trouble at home that is not your fault. Are your parents fighting, or considering separation and divorce? If your parents are divorced, are you having to adjust to living with just one parent? Is one of your parents remarried? Are you learning to live with a stepparent? Is someone in your family abusing drugs or alcohol? Is someone being sexually or physically abused? Has your father lost his job? Or gotten a job in a new city and you have to move? Is a family member very ill, or has someone died? Each of these is a circumstance over which you have no control, but which directly affects your life and your relationship with other members of your family.

What can you do, when there's trouble at home, to make things better for you and your family?

- *Be understanding.* Realize that *every* family has problems of one kind or another. Put yourself in your parents' shoes and try to imagine what you would do. Ask questions. Offer to help.

- *Respect confidences* within your family. When your parents confide in you and your brothers and sisters, they do so because they trust you. Do everything in your power to respect that trust.

- *Remain neutral.* You don't have to take sides. Fights between your parents usually have nothing to do with you. Of course they make you uncomfortable, but you can feel better by taking a walk, or playing your radio with earphones, or calling a friend. When the fight is over, talk to your parents as calmly as you can about how their fighting made you feel: "When you and Dad fight, I get scared that you are going to get a divorce."

- *Realize you aren't trapped.* Use friends, school, sports, volunteer work, odd jobs, and extracurricular activities to make up for some of the fun and happiness that are missing from home during troubled times.

Hints for Coping with Difficult Situations

It's always best if you can turn to your family for help when you have a problem—but it's not always possible. There are some important things you should know about some problems at home.

Divorce

Remember that your parents are not divorcing you. They are divorcing each other. You have a right to know where and with whom you will live, as well as who will take care of your schooling. Ask your parents these questions at a time when they seem to be calm and relaxed.

Stepparents and Stepfamilies

How do you treat a new stepparent or stepsibling? You treat them just as you would want to be treated if you were in their spot! It may not be easy, but they probably feel just as awkward as you do, so it's best to work it out together. If you're going to have to live together, it'll be easier if you try to get along.

Alcohol and Drug Abuse

Many teens have someone in their family who abuses alcohol or drugs. Treatment is available and possible for the abuser. Support groups such as Al-Anon are available for family members even if the abuser is not undergoing treatment. These groups keep information confidential and they can be extremely helpful.

Physical or Sexual Abuse

Obviously, if you or one of your brothers or sisters is being physically or sexually abused by one of your parents, you will have to ask another adult for help. Speak to your other parent, a trusted relative, or the school guidance counselor about it. It is not your fault if you are being abused. You are not a bad person. You have the right to say no to anyone who wants to touch any part of your body in a way that makes you uncomfortable. If they do it anyway, tell an adult whom you trust.

Death or Suicide

Most people feel angry when someone they love dies. You think, "How could Daddy leave me? I needed him." Or you feel guilty and you think, "Maybe if I had been there, it wouldn't have happened." Psychologists have done studies which show that everyone goes through five stages when someone they love dies: shock, denial, anger, guilt, and acceptance. So it's okay—even normal—for you to feel angry and guilty and sad, and you should realize that some of those feelings last for a long time. Share your feelings with family members; they're probably having the same thoughts and they, too, need to talk about them.

More information on all of these subjects is available in your school or public library. Don't be embarrassed to check out a book about divorce or abuse or anything else you are worried about. The librarian usually isn't paying attention, but you can always say you're writing a report on the subject if it will make you feel better.

Calling for Help

Sometimes when you feel you *must* talk to someone but have no one to turn to, the phone can be a real friend. Call the Information operator and ask if there is a crisis line in your town. They are ready to help you with any kind of problem. While there is no need for you to be embarrassed, that doesn't mean you won't feel that way when you first call. Try not to let your embarrassment keep you from calling. You'll find a caring and understanding person on the other end of the line who won't ask for your last name, or tell anyone about the call.

If you have a specific problem to talk about, you may find a listing in your phone book for suicide prevention, Alcoholics Anonymous or Al-Anon (for families of alcoholics), family planning, or venereal disease. Many of the organizations under these listings also have toll-free numbers that you can get by calling 1-800-555-1212 or using the toll-free directory at your public library.

Just remember that help is available—all you have to do is reach out for it.

6

Appearing in Public

WHEN YOU'RE IN PUBLIC

There are times when we're out in public and are confused as to what is the right or wrong thing to do. For example, what should you do when . . .

. . . *the elevator doors open?* Men and boys should let women and girls enter and leave an uncrowded elevator first. When it is crowded, the persons closest to the door exit first. The person closest to the "door open" button should hold it until everyone is through getting on and off the elevator.

. . . *entering a revolving door?* Men and boys should let women and girls enter first, but the men can help push from behind.

. . . *going through a pull door?* Men and boys should pull and hold the door open for women and girls to pass through first.

. . . *going through heavy push doors?* Men and boys should go through heavy doors first and hold them open for anyone coming behind. Never let go of a heavy push door without checking to see if anyone else is coming through directly behind you.

. . . *you feel the urge to write on bathroom doors and lunchroom tables?* Don't do it! Writing on public walls and property is inexcusable, and in some cases, against the law.

. . . *you've finished your meal in the car and there's no trash can nearby?* Hold on to your litter! In many states there is a stiff fine for littering. Don't take a chance—wait until you find a trash can.

. . . your posture isn't as nice as you'd like it to be? Lots of teens slump. They think it makes them look cool and casual. What it really does is make their stomachs poke out and their chests sink in! Now can you think of a single teenager who would *want* to have a flat chest and a fat stomach? *That's* why your mother tells you to stand up straight.

If you catch yourself slumping, here's a quick remedy: pull yourself up, as if you were a puppet with a string coming out of the very top of your head; then raise your shoulders and try to touch them to your earlobes. Get as close as you can, then let your shoulders drop. That is the natural position for your shoulders, not thrown back. Now you should look as comfortable as you feel.

Now that you're standing straight, see if you can walk while maintaining that good posture. Don't forget the string running up your spine and out the top of your head.

Pay attention to your feet. Are they making any noise? They shouldn't be if you're holding yourself correctly. If you catch yourself clumping, then watch yourself in a mirror while you walk and see what you're doing wrong. Chances are your body is racing itself to see which can get to the finish line first—your feet or your head. That's not what you want. All body parts are supposed to arrive in the same place at the same time! The same rules apply for going up and down stairs. Go lightly, not loudly.

Sitting is another thing that most teens (and many adults, too) have trouble doing properly. Sometimes you'd rather sprawl or drape yourselves on the furniture. We all like to do that sometimes, but you have to know when it's okay and when it isn't. It is okay to sprawl when you're in your own room alone. It is okay when you're in the family room with the family, if your parents don't mind. It's *not* okay when you are entertaining guests. It's not okay on the good furniture. It's not okay when you're visiting friends' or relatives' homes, even if they do it. It's not okay in public—at theaters, churches, rock concerts, restaurants, or any other public place you can think of. It is *never* proper to sit "Indian style" in a chair, and the front legs of the chair should *never* leave the floor.

Now that you know how you shouldn't sit, let's learn how you should. As you approach a chair to sit in it, turn and place the back of your leg against the front of the chair; then lower yourself into the chair using your thigh muscles only—no hands, no "plopping."

While sitting, keep your knees together and your feet on the floor. Hold yourself straight, but comfortable, resting against the back of the chair. You may cross your legs at the knee. Girls may also move their feet to the side and cross their legs at the ankle, which is really more attractive than crossing at the knee.

Boys may place the ankle of one leg on the knee of the other, as long as their back remains comfortably straight. When you are ready to get out of the chair, slide forward slightly and raise yourself to standing, using just your thigh muscles—no hands. This sounds a lot more complicated than it is. Make it a game and you'll get the hang of it in no time!

Confusion about how you should behave can also occur at concerts, movies, the theater, or when traveling.

AT A ROCK CONCERT

You didn't think there were any etiquette rules for rock concerts, did you? Even though your behavior is less restricted than at the movies or the theater (to put it mildly!), you should still show some consideration for those around you.

There seems to be a lot of moving through the aisles at rock concerts, especially while a not-too-exciting warm-up group is performing. Just try not to block anyone's vision, and be aware that if you stop, a guard or usher will ask you to move on—not to be mean, but to keep you from blocking fire exits, which is against the law.

When the main group or act appears, you may feel compelled to clap, sing, and dance. That's okay when everyone around you is doing the same thing, but pay attention to whether or not your actions seem to be annoying others.

If an adult or older teenager takes a group of teens to the concert, stay together or let the responsible person know where you're going. It's also a good idea to have a place to meet at the end of the concert in case someone gets separated from the group.

AT THE MOVIES

Because teens so often go to the movies in groups, it's important to stress the need for consideration toward others. It's okay
to hold a place in line for your date while he parks the car. It's
not okay to hold places in line for the vanload of ten people
who are planning to join you.

Once inside the theater, it's okay to sit together. It's not okay
to talk either to your date or to the movie screen, move con-
stantly, kick the back of the chair in front of you, put your feet
up on the chair in front of you, or wander back and forth to the
snack bar in a steady stream once the movie has started.

Because food is allowed in the movie theater, you must be
aware of the noise made by crumpling paper, popping gum,
slurping straws, or shaking candy boxes! If you've ever stepped
on a piece of discarded gum or spilled, sticky cola, you know
how helpful it is to put trash in the trash can instead of on the
floor.

Also remember that two heads together are twice as hard to
see around as one. Save your lovemaking for another, more
private, time and show consideration for those sitting behind
you.

AT THE THEATER, SYMPHONY, OR BALLET

Jason had such fun with Jennifer when they went to dinner
together that he decides to invite her to see a play. He gets the
tickets in advance and picks Jennifer up in plenty of time to
arrive ten minutes or so before curtain time.

When they reach the theater, Jason guides Jennifer ahead of
him as he gives both tickets to the person at the door and waits
for the return of the stubs. They'll be directed to the proper
aisle where an usher meets them, shows them to their seats,
and hands each of them a program. If the ushers are very busy,
Jason leads Jennifer down the aisle. Should Jason find someone sitting in what he believes to be their seats, he checks his
tickets and quietly says, "I believe you're sitting in our seats."
If this doesn't move the intruder, or should Jason have any
trouble finding his seats, he immediately returns to the aisle and

gives the tickets to an usher. Jennifer stands out of the way, next to an empty seat or in the aisle, until the problem is solved.

If Jennifer had the tickets and invited Jason to go with her, she would give them to him in advance. If the tickets were held for them at the box office, or if Jason were buying them at the theater, he would stand in line and Jennifer would wait out of the flow of traffic in the lobby.

When they reach their row, Jennifer goes first. If they're

double dating, one boy may go in first, then his date, then the other girl, and the second boy last. Girls often like this arrangement because they can talk between acts, but for this reason boys may prefer to alternate, sending one girl in first. Either way is correct.

If, in spite of all their planning, Jason and Jennifer arrive after the curtain has gone up, they wait at the back of the theater until the end of the first scene or until an usher indicates that they can be seated. Then they go quietly to their places. Or, if it's a musical, they may quietly slip into the row during the applause following a song and dance number. For late entry to a ballet or symphony, wait for direction from the usher to be seated.

If it's necessary for Jennifer and Jason to leave their seats either before or during intermission and their seats are not on the aisle, they simply say, "Excuse me," and wait for the others to let them pass. Those seated should stand and push their seats back to let Jennifer and Jason edge by. Nothing is more awkward than having to climb over someone who remains planted in his seat with knees drawn to one side—supposedly out of the way! Jennifer should make sure that her handbag doesn't swing against the heads of the people in the row in front as she enters or leaves her seat. To those they pass, Jennifer and Jason should say, "Thank you; I'm sorry to bother you."

AT A SPORTING EVENT

Football games and track meets are certainly more exciting with throngs of cheering fans. But don't let your excitement get out of hand. Be considerate of those around you.

Arrive on time so your neighbor doesn't miss the opening play because you're climbing over him to get to your seat.

Stop wherever you are and sing along or stand quietly when the national anthem is played. You may sit or continue your conversation as soon as it is over.

Shout and cheer when it's appropriate, but don't boo and hiss or you may find yourself the target of vicious remarks, or worse, from those around you.

When you jump up—and you will—in moments of excitement, hold on to your soft drink and popcorn so you don't dump them! Then sit down as soon as the excitement is over, or you'll be deluged with furious shouts of "Down in front!"

Walk, don't run, to the nearest exit when the event is over. If you don't have time to get out without shoving, then leave early.

WHEN PLAYING SPORTS

There is no question about it—being good at sports is an asset to any young person. But more important than being a good athlete is being a good sport. Some of the worst public behavior you'll ever see happens during sporting events. Please remember these points:

- *Temper tantrums* are immature and very unattractive. What do you think about someone who breaks a tennis racquet, throws a golf club or baseball bat, or argues with a referee?

- *Do your best* and play enthusiastically. Everyone likes to play with someone who appears to be having a good time.

- *Don't make lots of excuses* about your mistakes and don't dwell on your errors. A shrug of the shoulders or "I'm sorry, guys" will do.

- *Be sincere.* Comments such as "Oh, that's too bad—you almost made a hole in one" will seem insincere to your opponent. It would be better to say, "Doesn't it make you mad when you miss a close one?"

- *When you win,* give the loser a handshake and a positive comment like "It was a close match" or "You played a good game." The good winner, no matter by how wide a margin he has won or how poor a player he considers his opponent, should try to convince the loser that it has been a good match. If the winner can help the loser think that he or she has played a good game and has been fun to play against, he has succeeded in being a winner that everyone can applaud.

- *When you lose,* give the winner a handshake and a sincere "You played well." Swearing at your luck, making excuses, complaining about conditions, and, worst of all, protesting a decision by a referee or umpire get you nowhere except into trouble. Of course luck can be a factor; but in general, you lose because on that day you play an inferior game, and the test of a good loser is his being able to accept that loss and act as if he had enjoyed the match and played his best. You must be sincere in your congratulations.

Just remember that no matter which sport or sports you enjoy, you will have a better time and be more in demand as a partner or opponent if you show consideration, enthusiasm, and good sportsmanship.

WHEN TRAVELING

When you are traveling alone, it doesn't really matter how loudly you play the car radio or how many clothes you leave around your motel room. But when you travel with others, you must be considerate of them.

On a Plane

Arrive in plenty of time, usually thirty to forty-five minutes before departure, to check in and get your boarding pass and seat assignment.

If you have a good book, small quiet game, tape player with earphones, or handwork, bring it along. It helps pass the time.

Don't try to carry on any item that won't fit under the seat in front of you. If it's too big, check it!

Once you're on the plane, stay in your seat with seat belts fastened unless you *have* to get up.

Soft drinks, juice, and meals are free on most airplanes. You may ask for playing cards—some airlines give them away. Magazines are available for you to read, but you must leave them on the plane, except for the airline's own magazine, which you'll find in the seat pocket in front of you. There is no charge for taking that with you, but there is a charge for the earphones needed for stereo and movies.

Stay in the bathroom only the amount of time necessary and always leave it clean, whether you found it that way or not.

Remember that people are sitting very close together on an airplane. Talking loudly, playing your radio or tape machine so loudly it can be heard, and frequently turning your light on and off, moving your seat position, or raising and lowering your tray are all things that may annoy other passengers. Be extra sensitive to others in a plane.

In a Car

Whether you're traveling with family or friends, remember to buckle up.

Loud voices or radio playing are permissible only if other passengers agree.

Talk to someone only if they are receptive—don't talk to your sister if she's obviously absorbed in a good book, and never pick a fight with her while your mom is sleeping.

Sitting forward on the seat, lying on the back ledge, or holding hands and feet out the window is fun, but it's very dangerous and impossible to do if you're wearing your seat belt (hint, hint).

On a Bus

Travel on a bus is much the same as on a plane or in a car—close quarters call for super-consideration of others.

Keep your seat belt fastened (if there is one).

Changing seats while the bus is in motion is dangerous. A sharp turn while you're standing could send you flying down the aisle!

Sometimes eating is permitted. Check with the driver when you board, and remember not to litter.

When you are riding on a crowded city bus (or subway or streetcar), give your seat to an elderly person, someone who is handicapped, a mother with very young children, or someone with more packages than you're carrying.

In Hotels and Motels

Staying away from home is a treat, but you must consider others. Don't leave your manners behind when you travel.

Keep your shoes and clothes together in the hotel room. Your vacation may be cut short if someone trips and slips on your wet bathing suit on the bathroom floor and breaks a leg!

Running in the halls, playing on elevators or escalators or in revolving doors, playing the radio or TV too loudly, or jumping on beds is not permitted. Won't you be embarrassed if someone reports your behavior to the management or to your parents?

Towels, ashtrays, and ice buckets are not to be taken home. But it's okay to take soap, plastic shower caps, and laundry bags.

Around the Pool

Remember your safety and others' comfort when you're around the pool.

Walk, don't run.

Use plastic or styrofoam containers, not glass, around the pool.

Leave your towel on a chair or chaise only if you plan to return to it within twenty minutes.

Be aware of the noise you make. Some people sleep in the sun.

Look to see who's nearby before you do a cannonball into the swimming pool. Mothers with small babies and sleeping sunbathers don't want to be drenched!

Travel time is fun time. Just be sure you do your part to make it fun for everyone.

7

Entertaining

PARTY PLANNING

Even if you've never given a large party before, you've probably planned a number of small ones without realizing it. If you've had a few friends over to spend the night, watch a ball game, or swim, you've gotten permission from your parents, made sure there were plenty of snacks on hand, and given some thought to special activities.

Thinking in advance about problems that might occur is a sure way to prevent them. The more thinking, planning, and preparation you do before your party, the more fun you'll have attending it. Once the party is underway, you can relax and have fun!

Budget

The first question is, "How much can I spend?" Most of your money will be spent on food. But, depending on the type of party you want to have, you may also need to consider the cost of:

Invitations and postage
Entertainment—disc jockey, band, magician, clown?
Extra help—for cooking, serving, cleaning, lifeguarding?
Clothing—do you really need something new to wear?

Theme

Now that you know how much you can spend, what kind of party will you have? If your budget won't allow home-delivered pizza-parlor pizzas, then have a make-it-yourself pizza party. There are no limits to the kinds of parties you can have if you just put your imagination to work. There are dinner parties, dances, swimming, bowling or tennis parties, buffets, graduation parties, barbecues, beach parties, birthday parties, make-your-own pizza, ice cream sundae, hamburger, hot-dog, or sandwich parties, and of course, theme parties—Halloween, sweet sixteen, Christmas, Ground Hog Day, costume. Use your imagination!

Chaperones

Your parents will probably be more than happy to plan this part of the party for you, but you should have some input also. You and your parents (or whoever the chaperones are) should have a definite agreement on what will and will not be allowed—for example, no lights out, no refrigerator raiding, no liquor, no drugs, no fighting. The fact that chaperones are on hand does not mean that you are not to be trusted. They are there to help, if needed, and to protect your reputation and that of your friends.

At small informal parties, chaperones should be visible when guests arrive (which lets everybody know they are there), and then they should disappear to a bedroom or den. Rather than having them wander in and out to check on things, you should agree to call on them immediately if things get out of hand.

At large parties, the chaperones—usually the parents and their friends who have been enlisted to help—should stay in evidence. The refreshment table is a handy and natural place for them to congregate and make themselves useful.

Guests

The people you choose to invite to your party will be the most important decision you make. Will it be a "singles" party or dates? Will it be all girls or all boys? How many will you invite?

The number of guests you have will be influenced by the amount of space you have—if you want to have a formal dinner and your dining room seats twelve, then you'd better not invite any more than eleven for dinner (you make the twelfth)!

The success of your party will depend on the type of people you invite. If the party is very large, you can invite a number of different types of people, some outgoing, some shy, some who know lots of people, some who know only a few—they'll all blend together.

At a small party, try to have a good balance:

- Don't invite people who don't get along—the couple who broke up last week probably won't want to be forced to be together again quite so soon!
- Don't invite anyone to a dance or barbecue whose religion does not allow them to dance or eat the food you plan to serve.
- Don't invite eight talkers to a dinner party for eight—invite four talkers and four listeners.
- Don't invite a non-swimmer to a swimming party!
- Try to invite people who have, or who you think would have, something in common with each other.

Extra Help

If you've decided on a large party, you will need to think about whether or not you want to have extra help. Sometimes it's nice to have someone to help keep the glasses washed and the snack bowls filled. If your friends have their driver's licenses, you may want someone to direct people where to park their cars (just to be sure none of the neighbors' yards are ruined), or you might want someone to be on hand to change the music.

You can hire someone to do these tasks, a professional or a teenager in the neighborhood, or you can enlist the help of family members—maybe your older brother will take care of the music in return for your washing his car!

Food

The food for your party can be as simple or as elaborate as you like or can afford, but we'd suggest keeping it simple the first few times you entertain. Stick with things you know people will like and that you feel comfortable serving.

For snacks, chips, pretzels, popcorn, nuts, dips, cheeses, crackers, and soft drinks are always good choices. For informal meals such as cookouts and slumber parties, hamburgers, hot dogs, pizza, tacos, and spaghetti are better choices than short ribs, lamb chops, or baked fish. For sit-down dinners or buffets, you might choose items which can be prepared ahead and cooked while you're visiting with your guests, such as lasagna or baked boneless breast of chicken.

Your parents can help with suggestions for party food, but you will know more about what teens like.

Invitations

Invitations to any type of party may be issued by phone or in writing. Phone invitations are less expensive, but there are disadvantages—you may have to try several times before reaching some people, and once you talk to them you have no guarantee that they will remember your invitation because they have no written reminder.

Written invitations are a bit more trouble, but at least they supply your guest with the party particulars in writing. You can design your own invitations, buy fill-ins, or have them printed, but any invitation (phoned or written) must include the following information (not necessarily in this order):

Name (of those giving the party)
Date (day, month, date—for example, Saturday, July 25th)
Time (beginning and *ending*)
Place
Occasion (if it's a special one)
Clothes (casual or formal)
"R.s.v.p." or "Regrets only," accompanied by a phone number or
  an address (optional)

NOT THIS:

> *Jan and David [Jan who and David who?]*
> *invite you for swimming*
> *Saturday, May 30*
> *[where? what time?]*

THIS:

Jan Davidson and David Jansen
invite you for swimming, tennis, and a picnic supper
at The Cosmopolitan Country Club
on Saturday, May 30, at 4 o'clock

R.s.v.p. 343-4343
Bring swimsuit, towel,
tennis clothes, and your racquet.
Locker rooms available
for changing.

Mail written invitations so they are received at least ten days before the party. And be sure to respond promptly when you receive an invitation (see pages 35–37).

What to Wear

In the preceding invitation, the type of clothing you are expected to wear is fairly clear. Sometimes words like "casual" and "informal" can be confusing. We've included some general guidelines here, but never hesitate to check with the hostess when you're not sure. Remember, too, that any invitation is special, even if it's just to go to a movie with a friend. The more effort you make to show how much you appreciate being included, the more likely it is that you'll be issued another invitation.

Attire	*Boys*	*Girls*
Casual	Shorts or jeans T-shirts & sweaters	Shorts, jeans or pants T-shirts and sweaters
Informal	Sport coat and slacks with or without tie	Daytime dress or skirt and blouse
Semi-formal	Suit and tie or blue blazer with light slacks	Dressy dress or party dress
Formal	Black tie (tuxedo)	Evening dress

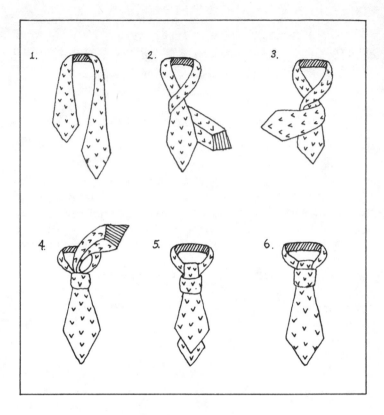

How to Tie a Four-in-Hand Knot

PARTY TIME

It's okay to be excited and just a little nervous. Here are some important things you can do to help everyone have a good time—including you!

Greeting Guests

Be ready a few minutes before the party is scheduled to begin so you can greet your guests as they arrive. You can ask any guest who arrives early to help with last-minute tasks. Introduce guests to others who may be arriving at the same time but whom they may not know. Make everyone feel welcome by smiling and acting truly glad to see them, then make a suggestion as to what they might do: "Coats and purses can go in the bedroom—food and punch are in the den. Make yourselves at home." For a small dinner party you might say, "I'm so glad you could come. Let me put your coat in the closet while you join Phil and Kathy in the living room. I'll be with you in a minute."

Just remember that your job as host is to put your guests at ease and they'll feel much more comfortable if they see you—a familiar face—when they arrive.

The Non-Mixers

At small come-on-over parties the problem of getting people to mix doesn't exist, but it certainly does when your group is big enough to include newcomers, or girls or boys who are not ordinarily members of your crowd. Walk among your guests at a party and try to spot those who appear to feel awkward or to be left alone.

At a dance, you can have your date or a good friend (or both!) ask an unaccompanied girl to dance. Introduce them by saying, "John is captain of the football team" or "Bill is visiting for the holidays." This can be a great help for someone who is shy and at a loss to know where to begin a conversation.

At just plain parties—some dancing, some chatting, some game playing—there are other things a host can do to help a sideliner. Get him or her involved by asking for help passing snacks or refilling drinks; sideliners will *have* to circulate to do that. Draw them into the conversation if you can, or ask their opinions on whatever you're talking about. When team games such as Ping Pong or volleyball are going on, be sure, even if you have to beg or bribe one of the captains, that the loners are chosen to play. As host or hostess, you must do your best for every guest, but you are not expected to continue "nursing" a loner all night. If, later, someone is still sitting alone, you can make one more try by asking him to join your own group for a snack, or by introducing her to a boy who is also something of a stranger. If that fails, you've done the best you can!

Party Problems

Most parties go just fine, but occasionally you run into a problem you didn't anticipate. Let's talk about a few.

Uninvited Guests

You should never let anyone into your home who is completely unknown to everyone there. This is most likely to happen at large "open house" type parties where "everyone's invited," and for this reason it's usually best to issue more specific invitations. Occasionally, though, guests of guests and friends of friends will show up at your parties. Your guests and friends should not invite others to your house without consulting you, but if the crashers are nice looking and well dressed, you may choose to let them stay. However, if there's no more room at the dinner table, or if the crashers don't know any of the guests or are inappropriately dressed, you should definitely send them away (even if you need the help of your parents to do so).

Drugs and Alcohol

As long as there are teenage parties, there will be kids who try to smuggle in liquor or drugs. This is *wrong*. In many of these cases it is not only wrong on moral and etiquette grounds—it is also against the law. You, as host or hostess, have the responsibility of preventing it from happening at your party. It's usually a fairly easy thing to spot. At regular intervals, a group of kids will leave the room. When they reappear, they probably act silly, smug, or guilty. That is when you act. You may tell your parents what you've seen and who is involved and let them handle it, or you can confront the culprits yourself. Without condemning or apologizing, tell them that liquor (or drugs) is *out*—you have promised your parents that there will be no drinking or pot, and the party will be cut short if there is.

Ask them for your sake, and that of your other guests, to turn over the stuff or leave. If they don't hand it over at once, tell them you're going to get your father, and, if there's still a delay, do it! Your father can back you up, and if the teens are underage, he should notify their parents.

Vandalism

Of course you hope that none of your friends would do anything destructive while they are at your house. But occasionally someone may decide to egg someone's windows, or let the air out of someone's tires, or write on the bathroom wall. Whenever you see this type of behavior, report it to your parents or the chaperones immediately. They have the authority to handle it and should be able to do so without the vandals knowing who reported them.

Making Out

There are ways to prevent it:

- Don't invite only couples who are going steady. It helps to have some guests who have something else in mind!
- Keep some lights on. Turn them low for sitting around the fire or dreamy dancing, but not all the way off. Your parents will object to total darkness, and you can use them as an excuse—"Look, I've got to keep one or two lights on. My dad said: no lights, no party."
- If the atmosphere seems dangerous, avoid too much mood music—change the songs from slow to fast!
- Keep plenty of refreshments flowing; you can always turn up the lights to pass a platter.
- If you have a steady date, discuss things with him or her in advance. Tell him you don't want your party to turn into an "orgy," and you might need his help. For that night at least, he must put romance out of his mind and behave the way you want the other couples to act.

Keeping the Curfew

It's the sign of a successful party when the guests don't want to go home, but eventually they must leave. When you issue an invitation, by phone or by mail, give a beginning *and* an ending time. That way, parents of non-drivers will show up to take them home, which will automatically start the breakup of the party. You may also allow the food and drink supply to run out about half an hour before quitting time. If it looks as though no one has any intention of leaving, get one of your best friends to help. "Mom and Dad are going to be furious if we don't break it up. Joe, would you mind starting the move?" If nothing else works, have your parents put in an appearance—that *always* works!

Being a Good Guest

A good guest should:

- R.s.v.p. or regret (if it is requested on the invitation) within one or two days after the invitation is received.
- Arrive on time for dinner parties or no more than fifteen minutes late for other parties. Never be early unless the host or hostess has requested it.
- Assist the host by talking to loners or introducing guests who don't know one another.
- Refrain from doing any of the things listed under "Party Problems"!
- Leave the party at the ending time, no matter how much fun you're having.
- Thank the host as you leave. It's also especially nice to make a thank-you call or send a thank-you note within a few days. After all, the host went to a lot of trouble to give the party—can't you spend a minute or two thanking him?

PARTY IDEAS

There is no limit to the number of reasons to have a party or to the types of parties you can give. Some people look for excuses to entertain—T.G.I.F. (Thank Goodness It's Friday) is a good reason to party, but so is T.G.I.M. and T.G.I.T. and T.G.I.W., etc., etc. Other people find entertaining more difficult. We'd like to give you some ideas that will be easy for you, no matter what kind of party-giver you are.

When entertaining, just remember this simple formula and you can't go wrong: Good Friends + Good Food = Good Times

Dinner Parties

These are probably the scariest parties for teens because you think, "I couldn't possibly invite friends over for dinner—what could I cook?'' Maybe you should think of them as supper parties; that sounds a lot less formal and a lot more fun.

Plan your menu around a theme. You can play up the theme with special invitations, decorations, and table settings, or you can use items that you normally use for nice family meals. Do make your table attractive, though, and save the paper plates, paper napkins, and plastic forks and cups for picnics and less formal occasions.

Dances

Parties which revolve around music and dancing are probably the most common type given by teenagers. They can be very simple or very elaborate.

A simple version might be held in the family garage (cleaned out, of course) or on the patio, with the host or hostess providing music from his or her own collection. Invitations would be phoned or handed out at school (discreetly, please, if you're not inviting the whole class), and refreshments would be easy items like popcorn, chips and dip, nuts, and soft drinks. Lights are turned low (but not off), maybe a few candles are lit for atmosphere, and friends dance and talk.

If you have a slightly larger budget, or maybe if you go in with a couple of other friends, you can hire a disc jockey to play the music. He usually has a better sound system (maybe you should warn your neighbors if you're planning this type of party), and he can get the party rolling by encouraging people to dance, announcing "ladies' choice" dances, and so on. You could have this type of dance in someone's family room or in the garage, but it could also be very nice combined with a picnic of hot dogs or hamburgers on the lawn or around the pool on a late summer afternoon.

The most elaborate and expensive version of the dance includes the hiring of a live band. You would probably want to hold this type of party at a school facility or a rented hall or country club. It could be casual, with everyone wearing shorts or jeans, or costume (maybe around Halloween), or dressy, with the girls in party dresses and the boys in coats and ties. For the more casual party, you would want to have more casual food. For the dressy party, you might want to serve finger sandwiches, pickup hors d'oeuvres and sweets, a hot item served in a chafing dish, and a pretty punch. Obviously, the more elaborate the party, the more expensive it is! Remember your budget.

Birthday Parties

Surprise parties are always fun, if everyone can keep it a secret. Clear the date with the birthday person's parents and tell them what you're doing so they can be sure to have the honoree in the right place at the right time. The surprise party can be a costume party, theme party, dance, or slumber party—whatever you'd like to do.

Tell guests it's a birthday party and help them by suggesting no gifts, silly gifts under a few dollars, or a dollar or two donation to a gift you know the guest of honor really wants. Sometimes the most special gift is Polaroid snapshots of the party, or an autograph book signed by all the guests.

Do have a birthday cake. Although everyone acts as if they think it's corny and the birthday person seems to die of embarrassment when "Happy Birthday" is sung, most people are secretly disappointed when this tradition is overlooked.

Christmas Parties

A Christmas party could be dancing under the mistletoe, or a lovely Christmas dinner, or time spent with friends making ornaments or wrapping gifts for a local nursing home. You might also consider Christmas caroling in your neighborhood followed by hot chocolate and cookies, or visiting underprivileged children (at a home for the retarded or a children's shelter) and entertaining them.

Halloween Parties

When you think of Halloween parties, you usually think of costume parties—but beware. Sometimes when people think they can't be recognized they misbehave, so keep everyone

busy with dancing, dunking for apples, and playing games. Scavenger hunts for frogs, spiders, crickets, and fireflies could keep everyone busy for a while!

Another fun variation on the costume party is to have everyone come as the same thing—vampire, ghost, or witch. Give a prize for the best costume and for the person that the fewest people recognized.

Other types of costume parties that can be given at Halloween or any time are:

Come as your favorite movie star.

Come as a famous pair—Fred Astaire and Ginger Rogers, Scarlett O'Hara and Rhett Butler, salt and pepper, King and Queen of Hearts, hamburger and french fries.

Come in your pajamas (but not indecent!).

Come in clothes from the 1950s or '60s, or '30s, or '40s.

Come as you were when you received this invitation.

Come as your favorite television commercial—cereal, soft drink, laundry detergent, toothpaste.

TV Parties

Get together to watch the Super Bowl, a World Series game, the Kentucky Derby, the Miss America Pageant, or the Academy Awards.

Provide everyone with pads and pencils and offer a prize for the best guess on the final score, order of finish, or whatever fits.

Put quilts on the floor in front of the TV and have a picnic! Serve cold fried chicken, potato salad, and baked beans on large sturdy paper plates.

After Skiing, After Skating, After the Ball Game

The main ingredients for these parties are a roaring fire and hot food and drink. You might have hot chocolate and hot dogs roasted over the fire, or hot apple cider and assorted sweet breads and rolls, or a mug of soup and toasted cheese sandwiches.

8

Dating Data

SHOWING YOUR INTEREST

Not too long ago, when a girl was interested in a boy there was nothing she could do but wait until he became interested in her. At one time just beginning a conversation with a boy was considered inappropriate behavior for a girl. It's a miracle that people with common interests found one another!

Luckily for you, times have changed. This is nice for the boys because it takes some of the pressure off them for always having to be the ones to initiate social activities with girls. It's nice for girls because it gives them an opportunity to develop friendships with boys—not just dating relationships. It's important to point out, though, that there is a fine line between being assertive and being obnoxious. Become the kind of person that others like to be around *without* calling attention to yourself by being noisy, or making trouble, or wearing strange clothes; *without* being too pushy—sending notes by all your friends, calling three times a day, or being there every time your heartthrob turns a corner; *without* relying on drugs or alcohol for courage. Most relationships don't last very long when one person starts out faking their feelings and being dishonest (which is what you do if you're high and trying to hide it).

Neither boys nor girls like to be harrassed by someone to whom they have politely made it clear that they are not interested. Remember that the fact that someone is not romantically interested in you doesn't mean they don't like you at all.

So how do you know what is enough and what is too much? How do you go about expressing an interest in that certain girl or boy? Begin by treating others the way you'd want them to treat you.

- *Be your best*—be the type of person people want to know. Look attractive—keep your hair, skin, and clothes neat and groomed.
- *Be honest,* but be kind. Your best friend just dyed her hair green and asks if you like it. If you hate it, try to refrain from saying that you now know what Martians must look like. Instead, tell her what you liked better about her regular color or style: "Green is definitely different, but I liked your hair better when it was red."
- *Don't gossip* or betray a confidence, or talk about others behind their backs. It can be hard not to go along when others start to gossip, but think how you'd feel if you learned others were talking about you behind your back.
- *Smile and speak.* Never be afraid to speak or say hello to anyone. Are you ever offended when someone speaks to you? Maybe you feel shy or are afraid that by speaking to that "certain person" he'll know you "like" him. If you smile and say hello to everyone, then no one person can feel they've been singled out and everyone just thinks you are friendly. Play a little game: make yourself smile and greet the people you pass in the hallways at school. Before long it will be a habit, and there will be a new, friendlier you—one whom other people will want to know more about!
- *Be interested.* Listen when others are talking to you and take an interest in what they have to say.
- *Develop common interests.* If he's in the business club, maybe you could join too. If you know she plays tennis after school each day, schedule a game on the adjoining court. Join church, school, or community organizations of which he is a member. The more often you run into each other (without being too obvious, of course), the more interests you have in common, the better the chances for a relationship to develop.
- *Arrange a meeting.* If the love of your life and one of your good friends have a class together, arrange for your friend to introduce the two of you. You might also have your friend arrange a blind (double) date, or invite you both to a small party.
- *Introduce yourself.* If his hall locker is right next to yours, or if you run into her often at the swimming pool, there's no reason why you can't introduce yourself. After talking for a minute or two, you'll have a better idea of what your chances are. Grumpy one-word replies aren't very encouraging, but cheerful, enthusiastic conversation should give you the courage to get to know each other a little better.

ASKING FOR A DATE

If you think, after you've met and talked, that he or she might be interested in you, why not ask for a date? We realize that this is not always as easy as it sounds, but here are a few tips to make it easier:

- *Ask early.* Two to four days before a regular date is sufficient, earlier for a special occasion. You're more likely to be accepted if the person you're asking doesn't feel that they're unpopular or a second choice.

- *Call or ask in person.* Don't send a note through a friend or have someone else ask—it looks as if you're afraid or don't have the confidence to do it yourself. Also, if you get turned down, you'll be glad no one else knows!

- *Use good timing.* Don't ask for a date when she's talking to a group of friends, or when he's in the middle of basketball practice. And if you want to make an impression on his or her parents, it's best not to call at the dinner hour or after 10 p.m.

- *Be specific.* Never ask, "What are you doing Saturday night?" Instead say, "Would you like to go to the movies Saturday night?" Once you've been accepted, be sure you give the time ("I'll pick you up at seven"), the transportation ("We're double dating with Paul and Diana in Paul's car"), and what to wear ("It's pretty casual—I'm wearing jeans"). If you have a curfew, be sure to mention it: "Is it okay if we go to the first feature? I have to be home by eleven-thirty."

- *Start slowly.* This is especially true for girls since boys are still getting used to the idea of girls asking for dates. Plan something that lets you hang around together, talk, and decide if you want to spend more time together. You want a chance to get to know each other better without spending too much time or money. Perhaps you could invite her to fly kites one weekend afternoon, or you could invite him and another couple over for pizza and a game of Trivial Pursuit. Sharing study time or working together on a school project is another good way to begin.

If the Answer Is Yes

Be enthusiastic and excited when accepting a date. After all, this is something you want to do or you wouldn't have said yes. If you can't give an immediate answer, state why: "My parents aren't home from work yet and I have to check with them. Can

I call you back in an hour?''

Once you've accepted a date, you *must* keep it unless you become ill or a family trip or situation requires your presence. If you wish, you may suggest another time or offer to try to find someone else to go in your place.

If the Answer Is No

Be honest about your refusal. If you're holding out for a better date, simply say, "I'm really sorry, but I already have plans." Then he won't be surprised if he sees you at the movies with another guy, or with another girl, or if he finds out you stayed home with your parents.

Refusing a date you'd really like to accept requires sincere regret so you'll be asked again. If the reason you must refuse is mentionable, give it: "Oh Scott, I'm *really* sorry but our family is going to my grandparents' house for the weekend. I'd love to have dinner with you another time." A reason that *is* true *sounds* true, and opens the door for him to ask you again.

If someone you aren't interested in dating persists in asking, it's probably better to tell him how you feel gently and honestly than to lead him on indefinitely. Just say, "You know, I don't think I'm the person for you, but I'm really flattered that you asked." Or you could say, "I think you're a really neat person, but my heart's with a guy in California." (Use this one *only* if it's true.)

Think before you refuse a date. After all, it only lasts a few hours, and you might really like each other. If not, you don't have to go out again.

If you do refuse a date, for whatever reason, keep it to yourself. Don't tell all your friends so they can have a good laugh behind his back, and don't tell Amy that the only reason she has a date with Scott on Saturday night is because you turned him down. Just remember how you'd feel if someone said those things about you.

NOW WHAT DO WE DO?

First dates don't *have* to be as awkward as they sometimes are. There are some things you can do to make it go more smoothly.

Fun Ideas for First Dates

Going to the movies is the most popular teen dating activity, but here are a few other suggestions:

- Miniature golf or a driving range
- Bowling
- Roller skating
- Ice skating—at a rink, or even better, on a pond if there's a full moon
- Dancing—Fast, slow, ballroom, and western or square dancing are all great fun if you know how. If you don't, lessons can be lots of fun too!
- Local plays or musical presentations
- Classes, lectures, seminars, and demonstrations, especially in college towns. Try a Chinese cooking class, karate demonstration, or a lecture on nature photography
- Church activities—You don't have to be a regular churchgoer to enjoy many of the activities planned by church youth groups.
- Sightseeing tours
- Museums and art galleries
- Horseback riding
- Fairs, carnivals, circuses, rodeos, and horse shows

Some of these won't appeal to you, and others may not be available in your town. But they may give you an idea or two, and you might have a surprisingly good time.

Look Your Best

Hang this list on your closet door and check it every time you dress.

Are you neat and clean?
Is your clothing appropriate for where you're going?
Is your outfit coordinated?
Are your socks and shoes appropriate to your outfit?
Are your shoes shined?
Is your appearance appropriate to your age?
Is your posture becoming?

Be On Time

Select what you're going to wear ahead of time and allow yourself plenty of time to get ready. Your date is probably as nervous as you are and will breathe a sigh of relief when you, not your father, answer the door. Being late could also cause you to miss the beginning of the concert, game, or movie, and that's no way to begin a date!

Introduce Your Parents

Tell your parents ahead of time your date's name and a little something about him so that they can start the conversation easily. Then when he arrives, take him to the kitchen, family room, or wherever they are and say, "Mom and Dad, this is Mitch Matchless." If possible, allow a few minutes of getting-acquainted time before you say, "Mitch, we'd better go if we're going to make the start of the movie," or whatever is appropriate. This little ceremony may not seem very important to you—in fact, it probably seems awkward—but it helps your parents feel more comfortable about who you're dating, and it proves to Mitch that you're proud of him and want to show him off to your parents.

Keep Your Parents Informed

Tell them where you're going and when you expect to be back . . . then call them if plans change. Don't they do the same for you? They probably won't need or use this information—and they shouldn't call just to check up on you—but it's important for them to have it if some emergency arises. Keeping them informed also builds trust. All you have to say is, "We're going to Cinema 4, and then to the Ice Cream Parlour for a sundae. See you around eleven o'clock." If you run into friends at the Ice Cream Parlour and decide to go to their house to listen to music, let your parents know.

Never sneak off to places your parents don't approve of with people you know they don't like. They'll surely punish you if they find out, but even worse, it destroys the trust you've earned.

Behave Appropriately

Since this is your first date, you'll probably want to impress the person you're with, but don't forget to be yourself—that's the person who got you this date in the first place! Until you get to know each other better, there are some subjects you should avoid—sex, gossip, dirty jokes, family secrets, and criticism of people or groups your date may know and like. Sitting too close or touching too much may imply that you want more physical closeness than you really do; be aware of the signals you send.

End on a Good Note

Some people spend their entire first date worrying about how to say goodnight. Boys feel that they are expected to attempt a kiss; girls feel pressured to comply. Don't worry about it—just do what you feel. Just because someone takes you out doesn't mean you owe them any physical favors; supposedly you were asked out because your date enjoys your company. A kiss on the cheek is a nice way to let a date know that you had a good time and would like to go out again. But if you're not comfortable kissing on the first date, thank your escort sincerely and say goodnight—don't linger at the door!

DATING DILEMMAS

Sometimes it's really hard to solve a problem when you're right in the middle of it—you just can't be objective. The basic rule of etiquette, to treat others as you would like them to treat you, can help solve many of the dilemmas of dating. You'd be surprised how many tight situations you can get yourself out of by answering, *honestly,* "How would I want to be treated in this situation?" Then act accordingly.

Blind Dates

For some reason, blind dates are usually considered dilemmas—"Should I go or not? What if he's a creep?" "What if she doesn't like me?" A blind date may seem a better option than sitting home, but you usually expect it to be a bore. Why not change the way you think about them? Accept blind dates, as long as they are arranged by someone you know, but go into them with the firm idea that they're only for one evening, and enjoy that evening as much as you can. If the date calls back, fine. If not, don't think you're a social flop—he, too, probably just wanted something to do for one night.

Peer Pressure

Peer pressure is exactly that—subtle pressure from people of our own age to behave or look the way they do. There is good peer pressure: to make good grades, to look attractive, to wash your car often. There is not-particularly-good peer pressure: to date at an early age, to go steady, to attend parties that you don't especially want to attend. And there is bad peer pressure: to drink alcohol when you're underage, to smoke marijuana or cigarettes, to use drugs, to have sex, to shoplift.

Some teens give in to the pressure in order to feel accepted. Great, if it makes you work harder for good grades, but not so great if it makes you get drunk every weekend. Other teens give in to the fear of not belonging by refusing to be pressured, which is great if it keeps you from shoplifting but not so great if it has you making C's when you could be making A's.

Think about the times you feel pressured. Ask yourself why you feel you need to go along with the group. We all want to be liked, but do you really want to risk being arrested for smoking marijuana just to get someone to like you? Is this really the type of person you want for a friend?

Remember that you always have a choice and you always have the right to say no. You *don't* have to do something that someone else wants you to do, especially if it doesn't feel right for you.

These choices are especially important to remember in a dating relationship. Because you care for someone, you are more likely to want to do things to please them—but beware of the person who seems to make unreasonable demands on you, and be aware of how those demands make you feel. Often, when we do something because someone else wants us to and not because we feel it's right for us, we end up resenting, or hating, or growing apart from the person that we feel "made" us do it. No one can make you do anything—the choice is yours.

Going Steady

Like everything else in life, going steady has its pros and cons. Let's look at them.

Pros	*Cons*
You don't have to worry about dates.	You're taken out of circulation.
You can feel at ease.	It can be boring.
You get to know each other better.	You get too involved.
It proves your feelings for one another	You feel pressured to have sex.
It makes you feel attractive.	It ties you down.
Everybody does it.	Everybody does it.

Before you say yes when that special someone asks you to go steady, ask yourself, "Why do I want to go with this person?" Perhaps you're tempted to say yes because your best friend is going steady and spending less time with you. Having a steady of your own would make you more like her and give you something to do in the time you used to spend with her. Is that a good enough reason to risk hurting someone else? Just be sure when you say yes that it's for the right reasons—the reasons that are best for everyone involved.

Breaking Up

It's very rare that two people want to break up at the same time, so usually one person ends up getting hurt. There's really no way to avoid that, but there are things you can do to make the pain a little easier.

Talk it over face to face. You'll be tempted to end it with a note or a phone call or a disappearing act because it's easier, but this is another case of not treating others the way you'd want them to treat you. Wouldn't you rather have a chance to ask questions and try to understand what went wrong?

Realize that there is real pain attached to love, so it's understandable that you feel hurt over a breakup. Express anger if you need to—pound your pillow, stomp your feet, have a long talk with your best friend—but be careful what you say and to whom. Remember, you really cared about this person once. An outward appearance of "It was great fun, but it was just one of those things" will get you over the hump and back into circulation.

Sex

It seems that sex is everywhere; advertisers use it to sell everything from toothpaste to diet colas, songs are written about it, and movies show all. It's no wonder that some of you think sex is no big deal. *Think again.* Sex is an expression of love between two people who really care for each other. It's not something you should do because:

"Everyone else" is doing it.
You want to prove to the guys what a "stud" you are.
You don't want to be a virgin anymore.
You want to know how it feels.
You want to be accepted or loved.
Your steady is pressuring you to.
You want to hold on to this relationship.

You guys should remember that girls usually equate sex with love; so if you have sex with someone, it's likely that she is going to expect more from the relationship. Are you ready to handle that responsibility?

Before you make the decision to have sex, ask yourself these questions and answer them *honestly.*

- Is everyone else *really* doing it—or are they just talking a lot?
- If I have sex with this person, will I be able to look him/her in the eye tomorrow and talk about the sexual experience openly?
- If it doesn't go well, how will I feel—embarrassed, angry, hurt, used?
- How will I feel if we break up afterwards anyway?

- What if this experience results in a venereal disease?
- What if this experience results in a pregnancy?
- Do I really trust this person?
- Do I like/love this person?
- Is this the *only* way to prove my love?

PDA (Public Display of Affection)

How do you feel when the couple in the back seat is going hot and heavy while you're trying to cool it with your date?

How do you feel when the couple in front of you at the movies is making out and blocking your view?

How do you feel when you take your little sister for a walk on the beach and you pass a couple kissing and groping each other?

How do you feel when you attend a party with someone you're dating for the first time and other couples are making out on the dance floor?

The way you feel about others in these situations is probably the same way they'd feel about you. Do you really want to make others feel angry, embarrassed, and uncomfortable? Do you want them to lose their respect for you? The decision is yours.

Drugs and Alcohol

If you are underage and your date tries to persuade you to drink or use drugs, *refuse*. It's against the law!

If your date gets too high to drive safely, get a friend to take you both home, or call someone (your parents, a taxi) to pick you up. *Never* allow someone who is high to drive, if you can prevent it, and *never* ride with a drunk driver. Which is more embarrassing: having your parents pick you up at the party or having them pick you up at the police station or the hospital emergency room?

Curfews

Most teens do have a curfew, but usually it varies depending on the occasion: you get to stay out later on weekends than week nights, later for special parties than regular dates. We hope that your parents discuss the time with you and that your curfew is a reasonable one. There will be times when you run late for reasons that can't be avoided—your car has a flat, the movie runs later than expected, or the party doesn't end on time. As soon as you realize you will be late, call your parents and explain the circumstances. If you aren't late too often, they'll probably be helpful and understanding when you are.

Dancing

Have you ever been at a party and had someone you didn't want to dance with ask you to dance? When that happens, there are three things you can do: (1) Dance. After all, it's not a commitment to marry, it's just a dance! (2) Say, "May I have a rain check? I was just on my way to the rest room." Then *go* to the rest room. You may *not* use this excuse and then dance with someone else. (3) Say, "I'm really thirsty. Instead of dancing, why don't we go get a soda?" Unless he refuses your offer, you must go together to get something to drink. Perhaps you can talk to a group of people and move away from this person gradually, but if he's really persistent and asks you to dance again after you've quenched your thirst, you must accept. You've probably noticed that unless the guy is really a lousy dancer, it's less painful and a lot faster to just go ahead and dance with him the first time he asks.

Gifts

It's fun to exchange gifts with someone you're dating regularly, but you should know that there are appropriate gifts and there are inappropriate gifts. Lingerie and underwear are never appropriate, no matter how long you've been dating. Very expensive gifts are inappropriate unless you've been dating for a very long time.

Always appropriate are: flowers and plants, books or a magazine subscription (of a respectable nature), cards (for any or no particular occasion), recorded music, a picture frame with a photograph of the giver, cologne, dinner out, or tickets to a special event.

Flowers

It is often a school custom to exchange flowers for special dances and proms. A boy should ask his date the color of her dress and then order flowers to match. He can give her a corsage to pin on her purse or to her dress at the shoulder or waist, a wristlet, which has band or ribbon to hold the flowers on her wrist, a nosegay (a small bunch of flowers to be carried), or flowers for her hair (if he knows her well enough to ask if this is what she'd like). She can give him a boutonniere (a small flower for the lapel), usually a rose or carnation.

If flowers are not customarily worn to school dances, a boy who wants to do something special for his date can send her a few flowers in a bud vase the day of the dance.

Budgeting

There is no question that dating is expensive, but if you're low on funds, you don't have to stay home alone. You can invite someone over for popcorn and television, to play board games like Monopoly, Scrabble, or Trivial Pursuit, to listen to music, to roast marshmallows, or to fly kites. You can go swimming at the club or a beach, have a picnic, go to a museum or the zoo, or go window shopping at the mall. Sometimes the least expensive dates turn out to be the most memorable.

9

Managing Your Money

Most teens feel that they never have enough money. As a matter of fact, most adults feel that way too! What about your own spending money?

WHERE IT COMES FROM

Allowance
This is how most teens get their spending money. If family finances allow, your allowance should fall in the same range as that of your friends. It's not good for you, simply because your family can afford it, to always be the one with more money than any one else. Neither is it good for you to have less than enough to pay your share or to go out with your friends, if your parents can afford enough for you to do so.

Gifts
Sometimes you get a nice little sum of money from relatives on your birthday or at Christmas or Hanukkah. You should never ask for money, but if they approach you for a suggestion, it's okay to say, "I'm saving up for a new sound system, so money would be helpful." It's also okay to tell your parents you'd like cash, in case they are asked for a gift suggestion. Unfortunately, you don't always know when you're going to get gifts of money, so you can't plan on them—but you can certainly enjoy them when they come!

Jobs

Sometimes jobs seem hard to come by if you're a young teen, but with a little creativity and hard work, you can earn extra money. This is definitely the best way to increase your income while making you feel really good about yourself. We'll talk more about jobs in the next chapter.

Borrowing

This is *not* the best way to get extra money. You should borrow only when it's absolutely necessary and when you're sure you can pay it back in a reasonable length of time.

WHERE IT GOES

Talk to your parents about what expenses your allowance is to cover—maybe it's only snacks and movies, or perhaps it includes dates and clothes. In either case, the challenge is to stay within your budget. If you get $20 a month for snacks, movies, and incidentals and you spend $10 on cologne at the beginning of the month, then you can only go to a couple of movies and have an ice cream cone during the rest of the month. *Think before you spend!*

Tipping

A hidden expense that we often forget about is tipping. Some teens don't realize that in many jobs (waiter, cab driver, hairdresser), the major part of an individual's income comes from tips. Others think that, because of their age, they do not have to tip. Should a waiter be penalized because he has been assigned to wait on you? Is it fair to expect the same service that an adult would if you are not prepared to pay at the same rate? (See pages 57–65 for some typical tipping situations.)

Admittedly, the practice of tipping occasionally gets out of hand, and there are times when you can refuse to tip—if the service has been really bad. But if it has been good, teenagers, like everyone else, must accept the responsibility of paying for it.

If you are ever in doubt about whether or not to tip for a particular service, watch those around you and follow their lead. There may be some variation according to where you live, but generally the following rules apply.

Waiters	15% of the bill before tax
	Some restaurants automatically add the tip (also called gratuity or service charge) to your check. Be careful that you don't tip twice!
Headwaiter	$5.00 if he rearranges tables to accommodate your group or performs other special services
	No tip is necessary if he simply shows you to your table
Room-service waiter	15% of the bill for each meal in addition to the hotel's set room-service charge
Checkroom attendant	25¢ when there is a charge for checking your coat
	50¢ per coat when there is no charge for the service and you check more than one coat
	$1.00 per coat when there is no charge for the service and you check only one coat
Washroom attendant	50¢ to $1.00 if the attendant hands you a towel or performs some other service for you
	No tip is necessary if the attendant does nothing for you
Strolling musician or pianist	$1.00 for playing a request
	Up to $5.00 for playing several requests
	No tip is necessary if you do not make a request
Lunch counter attendant	No less than 15¢ if you order only soda or coffee
	Otherwise, 10% of the bill, but never less than 25¢
Pizza or other take-out delivery service	$1.00 to $2.00, depending on difficulty of your order and distance of delivery
Parking attendant	50¢ when your car is brought to you
Shoe-shiner	50¢ for shoes
	$1.00 for boots

Taxi drivers	25¢ for a fare up to $1.50 15% of a higher fare
Airport porters or skycaps	50¢ per bag
Beauty salon owner-operator	no tip for shampoo and styling 10% of total bill for services other than shampoo and styling such as a perm or color No tip is necessary for any service in a shop where a "no tipping" sign is posted
Beauty salon operator	(when not an owner) 15% of the bill
Manicurist	50¢ to $1.00 (depending on the charge for the service and the fanciness of the shop)
Barber	25¢ to 50¢ in a rural town 50¢ to $1.00 in a city shop $1.00 to $2.00 if you are also having a shampoo, shave, or manicure

10

Job Data

So you want to earn some money. What do you do? Where do you begin? First you must consider some of the things that will determine the type of work you seek.

How old are you? If you are under seventeen, some states require you to get a work permit, often called "working papers." Your guidance counselor or school office may have all the information and application forms you'll need. If not, check the federal and state laws with your local Labor Department Office.

You'll need a Social Security number if you don't already have one. You can apply for one at any U.S. post office. The younger you are, the more creative you may have to be about your employment—some businesses are just not going to hire a fourteen-year-old, no matter how responsible you are.

Have you ever worked before? Really think before you answer this one. Perhaps you haven't worked for pay, but you probably have some experience that you can market. You may have mowed your own lawn for several years; why not begin a neighborhood lawn maintenance service, or consider working for a nursery or landscaping service? Maybe you've been babysitting since you were thirteen; why not do a summer camp for neighborhood kids at your house, or look into employment with a day care center or a local summer children's program.

Have you taken any classes that could be helpful to you in getting a job? Can you type? Do you know anything about computers? How are your filing and bookkeeping skills? Can you draw or paint? Do you know anything about car repair? Can you drive?

What are your interests? Do you like to meet people? Can you cook, or garden, or sew, or knit? Do you like selling? Do you enjoy writing stories, or reading, or drawing, or calligraphy? Are you interested in caring for the sick or elderly? Do you like athletics?

When you've really thought about your talents and abilities, you may have some idea of what kind of job you'd like. The next step is to get ideas from other sources.

- *Talk to your parents.* They know you best and will have helpful ideas about what you'll enjoy and be capable of doing. They may even have friends or business contacts who could be potential employers.
- *Discuss your interests and abilities with your school counselor;* he or she should be aware of job opportunities for teens.
- *Check the classified advertisements* in your local newspaper. Large companies and private individuals often find employees this way, and you may see something that appeals to you. You'll also notice that employment agencies advertise in the classifieds. If you get a job through an agency and the ad doesn't say "no fee," there will be a charge—usually a percentage of your first month's or year's salary—so you may want to consider this as a last resort.

Finally, after you've explored your options but before you've contacted potential employers, prepare a resumé—a history of yourself. This should be typewritten (if you can't type get someone to do it for you) and should include the following information:

- Name, address, telephone number
- Age, date of birth, Social Security number
- Diplomas or certificates received, if any, or last grade completed
- Courses related to the job you're applying for
- Interests and hobbies, especially if pertinent to the job you're seeking
- Past work experience, if any
- Names, addresses, and phone numbers of three people who would be willing to provide references. You may choose from previous employers, clergymen, teachers, and family friends, but before listing them, you *must* get their permission. You should not give family members as a reference.

With all the preliminaries out of the way, you must now decide whether you want to work for someone else or for yourself. Each choice has advantages and disadvantages. First let's investigate working for someone else.

WORKING FOR SOMEONE ELSE

Setting Up the Interview

Start early. If you're looking for summer or after-school and holiday employment, these are peak times and employers will have many applicants from whom to choose. If you're ahead of the crowd, you'll be more memorable.

Some job sources that are popular with teens, such as fast-food restaurants and grocery stores, do not require you to make an appointment for an interview. They usually conduct interviews at set times—Tuesdays and Thursdays between 2:00 and 4:00, for example. You can either pick up an application ahead of time and take it with you to the interview, or you can fill it out when you go.

Other businesses, such as department stores, take applications at any time. You simply go to the personnel department at your convenience, fill out an application, and meet with a personnel officer for an interview.

Most of the time, though, you are expected to call or write for an interview.

Calling is easy simply phone the personnel office, give them your name, and tell them that you'd like to set up an appointment for a job interview. You should then be given a date and time to appear.

Classified ads often give a post office box to write to for an interview, rather than a phone number. If you wish to make a good impression on a prospective employer, your letter must be neatly typed or written and must include all pertinent information.

Your street address
Your city, state, zip code
Month, date, year

Mr. John Fulmer, Personnel Manager
PREPS Clothing Store
P.O. Box 2051
Baton Rouge, LA 70808

Dear Mr. Fulmer,

In answer to your advertisement in the classified section of the *Morning Advocate,* I would like to apply for the position of sales clerk.

I am sixteen years old and a junior honor student at Episcopal High School. I enjoy being with people and like retail sales. For the past two years, I have led my class in the sale of Christmas greens—our school's annual fund-raiser. The guidance counselor at Episcopal High, Mrs. Steve Spaulding, would be happy to give you a reference. You may write to her in care of the school at P.O. Box 1234, Baton Rouge, LA 70816.

I have shopped at PREPS for several years and feel that I would very much enjoy working there. If you feel that I would be qualified to fill the position, please write to me at the above address, or call me at 344-4343, and I will be delighted to meet with you at your convenience.

Sincerely,
Leigh Graeber

The Interview Itself

Now that you have an appointment with your potential employer, remember to:

Dress Appropriately

Be sure that your hair and nails are clean and well-groomed. Your clothes should also be clean and pressed. A boy makes the best impression in slacks or trousers—not jeans—a shirt and tie, well-shined shoes or loafers, and a conservative sports jacket. A girl looks best in a nice skirt and blouse, suit, or tailored dress, hose, and shoes with medium heels (like something you might wear to church). Makeup and hairdo should not be too extreme nor clothes too tight.

Be On Time

You don't make a very good impression if you're late. When you arrive, go directly to the receptionist and state your name and the time of your appointment with Mr. Personnel. Then sit down and wait patiently until you are told to go in.

Take Your Resumé

Even if you are asked to fill out an application, your resumé will have needed information such as the addresses and phone numbers of references and your Social Security number. Never go to an interview without this information.

Remember Your Manners

Approach the interviewer with a smile and a firm handshake. Remain standing until you are told to sit; then sit in the chair indicated or one that is across from the interviewer. Do not chew gum, smoke, or fidget nervously.

Be Prepared

Let your interviewer direct the conversation, but when the lead is turned over to you, be ready with some intelligent questions about the training program, opportunities for advancement, and the work you would be doing. You may also ask about vacation time and pay, but only *after* you are sure you are interested in the work itself.

Remain Calm

Of course, this is easier said than done, but you'll make a better impression if you do. Sit comfortably in the chair but don't slump, and look your interviewer in the eye when you speak. Don't swing your leg, tap your feet, wring your hands, or do anything that will indicate that you are nervous.

Be Honest

The importance of honesty cannot be overestimated. Lying to make yourself look good can cost you your job if it is discovered. Also, many employers ask potential employees to undergo a lie detector test.

Thank the Interviewer

You can do this enthusiastically when you leave; you can also follow up with a short note thanking the interviewer for his or her kindness.

WORKING FOR YOURSELF

Maybe you will not be able to find employment, or perhaps you need a flexible schedule that only comes with being your own boss. Whatever the reason, here are a few suggestions to consider:

- *Lawn service*—mowing, edging, or gardening
- *Child care*—regular babysitting, or caring for children in your home and planning activities for them
- *Delivering newspapers*
- *Neighborhood newsletter*—sell ads to local businesses and get news from local residents, then publish weekly or biweekly
- *Services to the elderly*—reading aloud, writing letters, or running errands
- *Pet watching*—caring for pets for people who work or are out of town. Contact local veterinarians for referrals
- *Fix toys and bikes*
- *Wash and wax on wheels*—go to places of business or homes to wash and/or wax cars
- *Cake or cookie baking*—for any occasion
- *Disc jockey for parties*
- *Plan parties for children*—and assist the parents, or accept full responsibility for the party
- *Small painting jobs*—paint fences, dog houses, patio furniture, garage doors

- *Gift wrapping service*—your home or theirs
- *Ironing*—pick up clothes, prepare them for pressing, iron them, and return them to the customer
- *House sitting*—check on houses of people out of town: turn on lights, water plants, bring in newspapers, feed pets
- *Errand service*—run errands for people in your neighborhood

As you can see, there are lots of things you can do; but you must inform people of your service. Let them know by phone, community bulletin board, flyer, or postcard.

ON THE JOB

No matter what type of job you do, to be successful you must do it well. Be prompt. Be enthusiastic. Be cheerful. Be conscientious. Be courteous!

Index

About the Authors

Elizabeth L. Post is America's foremost etiquette authority today. Mrs. Post, granddaughter-in-law of the late Emily Post, revises the now classic *Emily Post's Etiquette* as well as writing a monthly column for *Good Housekeeping* magazine. Mrs. Post's other books include *Emily Post's Complete Book of Wedding Etiquette, Emily Post's Wedding Planner, The Complete Book of Entertaining from the Emily Post Institute* (written with Anthony Staffieri), *Emily Post on Weddings, Emily Post on Entertaining* and *Emily Post on Etiquette*. Mrs. Post divides her time between homes in Vermont and Florida. An avid golfer, she and her husband William Post are enjoying an active semiretirement with visits from their four children and seven grandchildren.

Joan M. Coles is an etiquette consultant from Baton Rouge, Louisiana, who also teaches manners and etiquette at the Emily Post Summer Camp.